D0993760

Stay Sharp
with the
Mind Doctor

To Fiona

Stay Sharp with the Mind Doctor

Practical Strategies to Boost Your Brain Power

Professor Ian Robertson

Vermilion
LONDON

1 3 5 7 9 10 8 6 4 2

Copyright © Ian Robertson 2005

Ian Robertson has asserted his moral right to be
identified as the author of this work in accordance
with the Copyright, Design and Patents Act 1988.

First published in the United Kingdom in 2005 by Vermilion,
an imprint of Ebury Publishing
Random House UK Ltd.
Random House
20 Vauxhall Bridge Road
London SW1V 2SA

Random House Australia (Pty) Limited
20 Alfred Street, Milsons Point, Sydney,
New South Wales 2061, Australia

Random House New Zealand Limited
18 Poland Road, Glenfield,
Auckland 10, New Zealand

Random House (Pty) Limited
Endulini, 5A Jubilee Road, Parktown 2193, South Africa

Random House UK Limited Reg. No. 954009
www.randomhouse.co.uk
Papers used by Vermilion are natural, recyclable products
made from wood grown in sustainable forests.

A CIP catalogue record is available for this book from the British Library.

ISBN: 0091902533

Designed and typeset by seagulls

Printed and bound in Great Britain by
Mackays of Chatham plc, Chatham, Kent

Contents

Introduction:
The New Prime of Life

How old do you feel?

So – you are over 50. People have very different attitudes to being over 50, irrespective of whether they are in their fifties, sixties, seventies or eighties. Would you describe yourself as:

1. Middle-aged?
2. Late middle-aged?
3. Old?
4. None of the above?

No matter what age you are between 50 and 80, the correct answer is four – none of the above. Why? Because terms such as '*middle-aged*' and '*old*' have lost their meaning owing to the dramatic changes that have taken place in our brains and bodies over the last generation.

These phrases emerged at a time when the average man retired at 65 and died at 70. Sixty was old and 50 was very late middle-aged. All this has changed. Some people retire at 50, others at 80. Homemakers don't retire at all. What's more, the whole notion of 'retirement' – with its connotations of gold watches and prize marrows – has changed beyond recognition. Many of us will choose to keep working into our seventies; equally, many of us will be obliged to.

If you are 50 and living in a Western country, then you can expect to live *on average* for another 30 years – until you are 80. Remember, however, this is an *average* that includes smokers and people with poor diet and exercise patterns. If you are a non-smoking 50 year old who eats well and takes regular exercise, you can expect *on average* to live significantly longer than another 30 years.

For people with a healthy lifestyle then, true old age – with its connotations of frailty, disability and illness – tends to kick in sometime after the age of 80, or even later. Of course there are exceptions to this, and women tend to do better than men. But the fact is that when you turn 50, you have a reasonable expectation, on average, of 30 more years ahead of you – a period longer than youth.

In 1984, I began studying the effects of ageing on the brain and how to reverse them. One group of people I worked with had suffered a stroke. At that time, the average age of those admitted to hospital with a stroke was around 72.

By 1999, the average age of my stroke patients was around 82. In just 15 years, I saw with my own eyes how people had become physically 'younger' by roughly 10 years.

How on earth could this happen? – Better diet, less smoking, more exercise and better monitoring and control of blood pressure were some of the more important reasons. But it wasn't just the average age of stroke patients that had changed – the ordinary people around me who were 50, 60 and 70 were all looking – and behaving – younger as well.

I saw this in particular in the volunteers who came to my laboratory in the Cognition and Brain Sciences Unit, in Chaucer Road, Cambridge. These men and women were part of our so-called 'participant panel' of people who offered their services in helping us understand how and why the brain ages. Many of them were retired from formal employment, and had the time and inclination to help our scientific research.

What was striking about these men and women was that they looked, on average, about 10 years younger than their chronological age. To a man and woman they were bright-eyed, intellectually curious, usually physically fit, and with a healthy sheen to their often tanned skin. Notably, it was often hard to pin them down for their next appointment – they had full diaries.

They were a difficult bunch, I have to say. Not truculent or anything – but just a bit too smart for the good of our research. We wanted to measure and study the effects of normal ageing on memory, thinking, concentration and so on, but these people were, by and large, just too damned good. We found it hard to repeat with them some of the find-ings from other parts of the world that had shown how people became less mentally sharp as they get older.

Then the penny dropped: many of these studies were 10 years old. And they were often carried out in places where

HOW PEOPLE ARE GETTING YOUNGER

Since the 1950s, life expectancy has increased by eight to 10 years. A 60-year-old woman in the UK, for instance, can expect to live, on average, until the age of 83 and a man to just under 80. Life expectancy in Europe was only 22 years at the time of the Roman Empire, 35 at the beginning of the nineteenth century, and 50 at the beginning of the twentieth century. Our concept of what constitutes middle versus old age was formed decades ago, and has not caught up with the fact that we are becoming biologically and mentally younger each decade. This is becoming increasingly important, given that, for instance, by 2025, one in four Europeans will be over 65. There will be 70 million Americans over 65. It is estimated that, by 2050, to maintain current levels of pensions, retirement age in France will have to be 78 and in the US 75. Improved health care, diet, living conditions and reductions in smoking are among the reasons for this. But the key thing to remember is that 50–80 period of life is no longer what it was!

people did not cycle in for their appointments, have active lives, eat good diets, avoid smoking and learn foreign languages in their seventies. In other words, the people being studied were not as 'physically' young as they were in Cambridge.

Most of us are 10 years younger than we think we are

If you keep yourself reasonably healthy, there's a good chance that you are biologically younger than your parents were at your age. Yet many of us – consciously or unconsciously – have in mind an image of what being 50, 60, 70 or 80 *means* that hasn't kept up with the positive changes that have occurred in our bodies and brains. Mentally, we tend to base our expectations of how we should behave and what we should expect out of life on our memories of our parents and grandparents.

Generally, therefore, we should think of ourselves as, potentially, being a decade younger than we actually are.

If you smoke, have a bad diet, don't take exercise, have untreated high blood pressure or a chronic disease, this might not necessarily apply to you. But otherwise, you really should consider yourself as 10 years more youthful than your birth certificate declares.

So let's go back to my first question: Do you think of yourself as middle-aged, late middle-aged or old?

Do you refuse to answer on the grounds that these are out-of-date categories based on a human biology that no longer pertains? Excellent!

So let's formally dump the three ages of man and replace them with four.

 YOUNG – 0-25: Can be fun, but tough going. You have to learn the most incredible amount of stuff. They don't pay you much – or at all – and you can't be certain that they ever will. By your mid twenties your brain is just about fully wired up, so if you haven't killed yourself by impulsive driving or dangerous drug usage, you are in reasonable shape for the next part of the journey.

MATURE - 26-50: Hmm, mortgages, insurance, careers, families, money. This stage of life can be stressful, but also pretty joyful. But what's the biggest bugbear? Time. There just isn't enough of it.

 PRIME - 51-79: A period longer than youth, but with a freedom potentially greater than youth. Freedom from the need to prove yourself, whether in exams or relationships. Opportunity to change, to develop yourself in ways that didn't occur to you or were barred to you when you were younger. But most of all, you have – time. Of course, this is not inevitable. Finances, health or family commitments might limit your choices – but that is true at any age. Such limitations never eliminate the choices you have in the new prime of life.

 OLD - 80-100: The 10-years-younger rule is based on an *average*. There are many super-young 80 and even 90 year olds – and these numbers are growing. Being old has its own compensations and opportunities.

You may not be as old as you feel

How old we feel depends largely on how old we *think* we are. But our thinking is influenced hugely by the *language* we use. The language we use to talk about age, however, is out of date. It is like talking about the Internet using the terminology of carrier pigeons.

You can feel old because you think you are old. And you can think you are old because you apply words to your chronological age that no longer apply. Feeling less old involves a number of things, including taking more exercise, eating healthily, keeping your blood pressure normal and stopping smoking. But is that enough?

Just as the body needs exercise, so does the brain. It needs both general exercise (new learning, challenge, new skills) as well as *specific* mental training to get the very best out of it. Later, you'll see how mental training can reduce your cognitive age by up to 14 years. In other words, 70 year olds can be trained to have the mental capacity of 56 year olds.

Just as importantly, you need to learn new *habits* of thinking about yourself and your stage of life. Thinking young isn't just a matter of saying to yourself, 'Okay, I'm actually 10 years younger than my passport says.' As you'll see in the next chapter, our age self-concept is shaped mainly by *unconscious* processes: thousands of moulding presses of life's sculptor that shape your age-view of yourself into a hardened statue.

If you want to remould that statue, you have to work at it. That is what this book is about.

You may be in your fifties, sixties, seventies, eighties or older. Here are some notes for your age group as to why and how you might use this book.

Fifties You may still be doing the same job – whether in a workplace or at home – that you have been doing for the last couple of decades. But you can see changes on the horizon – organisational change, your family dispersing, retirement, redundancy – or the simple feeling that you don't want to go on doing what you are doing indefinitely.

This is potentially a very exciting time. This could be the beginning of your prime – a second youth that is both longer than youth and potentially much less stressful. You have so many opportunities. But to grasp these opportunities you *must* be mentally sharp.

 Sixties For most people, the end to a formal career is looming large, if not already here. If you have been working at home with the family, your children are now adults. Like it or not, change is upon you. Change can disturb – even damage – unless you embrace it.

A sense of *control* is of the essence here. Being swept down the rapids in a boat is terrifying. Steering the same boat down the same rapids can be exhilarating – but only if you have learned to steer. This book teaches you how to steer, and how to develop the mental abilities and attitudes to be able to steer well.

It's really very important to start to develop the habits of thought that will keep you mentally young. New habits are easier to acquire the younger you are. This is because learning is a *habit* and a *skill*.

We learn an awful lot in our teens and twenties, but tend to rest on our laurels in our fifties and sixties. Part of the reason that the young can be smarter is because they are *used to learning*. This book will help you to gain the mental sharpness that will help you to make the very most of this exciting second decade of the prime of life.

Seventies This can be a great time. You don't necessarily care what other people think of you. You can throw off the self-imposed limitations of your younger self-image. You can do anything now. If you are healthy, this can be a very sweet time of life indeed. But to enjoy it, it is absolutely crucial that you carry out a major service on your brain: that is what this book offers.

Research shows[1] that you can reduce your cognitive age – in terms of memory, thinking, mental speed and concentration – *by up to 14 years* by practising the kinds of exercises that you will learn about later in this book.

🔆 **Eighties and over** You may be sharper and smarter at 80+ than others are in their fifties. You may have decided that you want to enjoy a very relaxed old age and do not want to be bothered with new learning, new mental habits or changing the sculpture of your self-concept. This is absolutely understandable when you are over 80, but not for everyone. Some over-eighties still have a hunger for new challenges and new learning. For them, mental sharpness is essential.

But who am I to write such a book, and why should you believe me? I am a 53-year-old neuropsychologist and university professor. I have studied how the human brain is physically changed by experience – how 'use it or lose it' is a fact, not a myth. I have published research showing how it is possible to improve brain function through the right kind of training[2]. My book *Mind Sculpture* showed how our brains at any age can be moulded by experience[3]. I decided to write this book to help people put into practice the scientific facts described in *Mind Sculpture*.

Whether you are in your prime or in your old age, I wish

you good luck in developing your mental sharpness through the following 10 steps, and in putting this sharpness to use in enjoying the new prime of life.

How to use this book

This is a 10-step programme which, if you put it into action, will significantly increase your mental sharpness and reduce your cognitive age. The first two steps help you *assess* your own thinking about your age and to work out whether your lifestyle could be ageing you. The remaining eight steps help you to put into action a plan that deals in turn with:

- ☼ Stimulating your brain through building challenge in your life.
- ☼ Stimulating your brain through increasing change in your life.
- ☼ Building your brain by increasing learning.
- ☼ Increasing motivation to build mental sharpness.
- ☼ Boosting your mental functions through exercise and diet.
- ☼ Reducing stress and learning to relax.
- ☼ Improving your memory.
- ☼ Improving your mind management.

Read through the book first and then come back to the steps that most appeal to you. Good luck in sharpening your mind and brain!

Step 1:
Measure Your Think-age

Two men

The first man is 52, a middle manager. He has been working in the same company for 24 years. He has driven the same route to work for 24 years. He is mildly bored with his job, but is good at it. Experience and delegation get him through the working day. It is years since he encountered anything he hadn't come across before, and he is senior enough to be able to delegate the learning of new technologies or procedures to his staff. His social life is equally comfortable and unchallenging – one of high predictability and routine. The same groups meet for dinner on roughly the same weekend year after year. Weekends away are programmed and predictable years in advance. He dresses conservatively and functionally. Food to him is fuel rather than enjoyment, but he loves his garden – this is his main form of exercise. He is only slightly overweight. Life is pleasant but he often talks about how he hopes to get a 'package' when he is around 58.

The second man is 62. He was made redundant in his late fifties. At first, he was shocked and disoriented, but after a while he began to enjoy the freedom that came with no longer being a company man. He began to travel, and when he was offered consultancy work, felt ambivalent about giving up some of his new-found free time. This work took him abroad, and he loved the experience of living in a continental European country, albeit part time. He started to take an interest in food, wine, cooking and clothes. He dressed in a more fashionable and stylish way. His tastes in music developed and he made new friends who were from backgrounds quite different from those of his long-established acquaintances. He joined a gym, lost weight, and replaced his old-fashioned pudding-bowl haircut with a more trendy one.

The 62 year old looks and behaves younger than the 52 year old. What's more, they are one and the same person. He is someone whom I watched clawing back the 10 years that all of us can aim for, spurred on by the shock of redundancy. It's not something he did overnight – it took an extended period for him to remould the sculpture of his self-concept and to match his mental age with his biological potential.

Your age and your unconscious

Most of what we do is shaped by largely unconscious habits, thoughts and feelings – including how old we behave and feel.

Take as an example the following study by the eminent social psychologist John Bargh[4]. Volunteers came to his office to take part. Half of the volunteers had to unscramble mixed-up sentences that included terms related to conventional stereotypes about the elderly, such as 'wrinkle', 'grey', 'wise'. The other volunteers sorted sentences that included no such words.

The volunteers then left the room. As far as they were concerned, the study was finished. In fact it was still going on. Professor Bargh's video camera was trained on them as they walked from his office to the lift in order to measure how fast they moved. The results were startling.

The volunteers who had sorted the sentences that included words linked to ageing walked *slower* than those who had read the alternative material. But the first group had absolutely no awareness that they were doing so. The mere fact that their brains had been exposed to ideas and thoughts about old age affected how fast they walked.

If just a few minutes spent reading can change how you behave, imagine the effects on you of decades of thinking old, and immersing yourself in experiences linked to age.

This, of course, is not about chronological age. There are many chronologically old people who are mentally young, and it can be more rejuvenating to mix with them than with juniors who behave old.

Remember, you can make yourself mentally younger by casting off out-of-date notions about middle- and old age. But this isn't just a question of saying, 'Okay, I'll think young'. Why? Because our self-concept of how old we are is sculpted by thousands of habits of behaviour and thought, most of which we are quite unaware of.

It's a bit like trying to learn to play golf properly, after you have played for years using self-taught bad habits. It will take months for a coach to help you unlearn your bad habits and learn the new ones that will boost your game.

The point here is that growing older is as much a state of mind as it is a biological reality. At every age our brains are physically moulded by experience. What we experience is, in turn, shaped by our self-image: if we feel old and stale, we behave old and stale, and our brain is thus starved of brain-growing stimulation.

Change can only happen if you make yourself aware of the habits you want to change. Shortly we'll start with your analysis of how old you behave and think. If you haven't read my

HOW YOUR BRAIN IS CHANGED
BY WHAT YOU THINK AND DO

Memories, skills and experiences are embroidered into a network of up to one hundred billion brain cells. On average, each of these brain cells is connected a thousand times with other neurones, making a total of one hundred thousand billion connections. This exceeds the number of stars in our galaxy.

The meeting point between two cells is called a synapse and a brain cell is shaped a bit like an onion, with a roundish middle, a single long shoot at one end, and lots of thinner root-like fibres sticking out of the other. An onion sucks up nutrients from the ground, processes them in the onion and sends the results up into the sprouting shoot, and brain cells work a bit like this, too.

The cluster of thin fibres converging on the brain cell

corresponding to the onion's roots are called 'dendrites'. Like the roots of the onion, these dendrites suck up nutrition into the brain cell. But the particular 'nutrition' which they bring consists of electro-chemical impulses from other brain cells.

And the single long shoot on the brain cell is its 'axon'. Brain and nerve cells have a single axon, which are their only channel into the rest of the brain. Axons can range in length from a tenth of a millimetre to two metres. When the brain cell sends a signal down its axon, it does so in a single blurting pulse, not a constant trickle. This pulse lasts about a thousandth of a second, and travels at a speed of anything from 2–200mph.

The pulse travels down the axon where it comes into contact with the dendrites of another brain cell. That point of contact is the synapse. This continues through the trembling web of neurones, connected by synapses. And so a chain reaction occurs, with cells firing off in their hundreds, thousands or millions across the three dimensional net.

So, at this very moment, as you read this sentence, a cascade of electrical brain cell activity is happening in your brain, across these all-important junctions – the synapses. The experience of reading these words is physically re-shaping your brain at this moment, sculpting the network of connections into new patterns.

By giving your brain new experiences, challenges and learning, you help build better connected webs of brain cells, and so improve brain function at this crucial time in your life. This book teaches you how to do this.

earlier book, *Mind Sculpture*, the box on pages 14–15 explains how your brain is physically moulded by experience.

Assess your think-age

Your 'think-age' is how old you behave, irrespective of how old you are. It's a strange fact but true that the way we think and feel is influenced hugely by how we behave. Before starting the programme, try the exercise in the box below, 'Why a smile can make you happier'. This explains how habits of

WHY A SMILE CAN MAKE YOU HAPPIER

Try this exercise. Pull your mouth up at the sides into the shape of a smile and hold it there for 20 seconds. On average, this trivial act slightly improves mood (though it may not be apparent in your particular case in such a short time). This is because making the shape of a smile causes a pattern of muscle activity in the face that connects with a particular pattern of brain activity. Because simultaneous activity in different brain areas tends to link up these areas, then a chain reaction is set up between the movements of your face muscles and patterns of activity throughout your brain.

At the end of this chain reaction is the brain activity associated with happy, positive feelings, deep in the emotional centres of your brain. Because 'cells that fire together, wire together', and because these facial muscle movements have been linked to happy feelings hundreds of thousands of times before, then moving your mouth into that position causes a small increase in positive-emotion-related brain activity deep in your brain.

behaviour feed back into our brains and change how we feel and think.

'Behaving our age' follows the same principles. Of course there are limits: you wouldn't want a 50 year old behaving like a five year old, or vice versa. But in the new biological world that we have entered, the old associations between particular patterns of behaviour on the one hand, and particular decades on the other, have become much looser.

Yet these associations linger on not only as attitudes and expectations in our brains, but more importantly as habits or patterns of behaviour. To give yourself the chance to win back extra mental years, you have to carry out an audit of your own 'think-age'. Start by answering these questions:

Do you often mention your age to friends or colleagues?
Yes ❑ No ❑

Do you believe that you are too old to change much?
Yes ❑ No ❑

Do you sometimes give up on mental tasks (such as mental arithmetic) that you used to be able to do?
Yes ❑ No ❑

Do you rule yourself out of certain situations or activities (for instance, taking up a new activity or job) because of your age?
Yes ❑ No ❑

Do you often find yourself thinking about your age?
Yes ❑ No ❑

Do you complain about your memory?
Yes ❑ No ❑

Do you find yourself groaning when you bend down?
Yes ❑ No ❑

Do you now catch yourself stooping as you walk?

Yes ❏ No ❏

Do you avoid buying certain clothes that appeal to you because they are 'too young'?

Yes ❏ No ❏

Do you sometimes have the feeling that all the new, unfamiliar and exciting experiences in life are behind you, and that the future is largely one of familiar routine?

Yes ❏ No ❏

Score your 'thing-age'. Give yourself one point for each 'yes.'

7-10: Your think-age score is high. You think yourself much older than you need to. You tend to feel your age (whatever that means!), which implies, probably, that deep down you feel old. Assuming that you are not sick, your behaviour pattern consists of a set of habits that are not necessarily linked to your chronological age. You have picked up a lot of the stereotypical baggage associated with age in the form of deeply-ingrained habits of thought and behaviour. None of these habits is in any way necessary, yet they age you as surely as the years. They reflect a – probably unconscious – self-image of yourself as someone who is old – maybe even 'past it'. You need to spot each one and kill it before it gets you. Read on.

4-6: You have a reasonably strong propensity to think old, but you haven't developed the full portfolio of unnecessary habits linked with the stereotype of age. From time to time you still feel old, however, and there are still a number of well-embedded thinking patterns and habits of behaviour associated with your unconscious assumptions about your age. You need to spot these habits and exterminate them before they spread.

0-3: You tend to think young and have avoided picking up much of the unnecessary baggage of 'old-think'. It is important, however, that you continue to avoid picking up habits and thinking patterns linked to old-think in the future. Sometimes a shock, like redundancy or a child leaving home, can drastically alter a person's way of thinking.

How old is your lifestyle?

Your lifestyle is a big factor in your think-age. I showed you earlier how we pick up age-habits quite unconsciously simply by coming into contact with words and images that are linked to conventional notions of old age. It follows that if you spend a lot of time with people who are mentally old, and not much time with mentally youthful people, you will unconsciously pick up habits linked to mental old age.

But remember, this has nothing to do with chronological age – some of the mentally youngest people I have met are in their eighties, while some of the mentally oldest are in their forties!

Your lifestyle is an important shaper of your mental age. Let's have a look at how old your lifestyle is. Answer these questions.

In the last three months, have you done something that you had never done before?   Yes ❑ No ❑

In the last year, have you learned something completely new (such as a skill, a song, a hobby or a body of knowledge)?

Yes ☐ No ☐

Have you deliberately taken any exercise in the last week (such as a long walk at a brisk pace, rather than a stroll to the shops)?

Yes ☐ No ☐

In the last month, have you had – outside of normal work – a conversation with someone you had never talked to before?

Yes ☐ No ☐

In the last month, have you deliberately listened to music of a genre you had not listened to before (such as jazz, classical, rap, opera, techno, country and western – anything you are not used to)?

Yes ☐ No ☐

In the last month, have you read a book of a genre that you don't normally read (such as a thriller, romance, biography, popular science work, hobby, cookery, gardening, sci-fi)?

Yes ☐ No ☐

In the last month, have you gone somewhere within easy reach of your home or work that you had not been to before (such as a park close to your workplace, or a café near your house that is on a road you normally don't walk down)?

Yes ☐ No ☐

In the last three months, have you done something out of your routine utterly on a whim?

Yes ☐ No ☐

In the last month, have you gone to bed much later than usual (for example, staying up to watch a film, read a book or listen to music)?

Yes ☐ No ☐

In the last month, have you got out of bed much earlier than usual for a positive reason (such as going for a non-routine early-morning walk, or just to watch the dawn while having breakfast)?   Yes ☐ No ☐

In the last three months, have you taken action about something that had been bothering you for some time but which wasn't part of your normal routine (such as fixing a cupboard door or buying a new shrub for the garden)?   Yes ☐ No ☐

In the last three months, have you done something out of the ordinary at lunchtime (such as going to a concert, walking in the park, visiting an exhibition or trying something new to eat)?   Yes ☐ No ☐

Score your lifestyle age. Give yourself one point for each 'Yes'. What was your score?

9-12: Congratulations. You are reducing the risk of unconsciously picking up the habits of old 'think-age' by keeping your lifestyle flexible and fresh. You'll find that life doesn't flash by so quickly when you break out of routine and sample new experiences.

6-8: Not too bad. You break out of routine to a reasonable degree. But you still have scope to adopt a younger lifestyle by building in more change and novelty. These changes will reduce the risk of your unconsciously picking up thinking habits and behaviour patterns that will push you into an old-age frame of mind.

4-7: It really would be worth your while including more novelty and change in your lifestyle. Maybe you feel you are too busy, or too tired, or too stressed. But the fact is that feelings of pressure, fatigue and stress can be a symptom of a stale lifestyle as much as a cause of it.

0-3: It's great that you are reading this book, because that means you recognise that something should change. Congratulations. But the fact is that your lifestyle is putting you at risk of thinking and behaving old. You will be more likely to mix with people like yourself, who are caught up in fixed routines. This will limit the conversations, experiences, ideas and emotions that you have.

So, in this first step of your programme, you have analysed your 'think-age' and also assessed whether your lifestyle could be ageing you unnecessarily.

In the next chapter, Step 2 of your programme is to analyse your lifestyle in more detail and to consider why you should boost your mental sharpness.

Step 2:
Is Your Way of Life Ageing You?

The young rebel

In 1963, the artist Pablo Picasso developed a radically new style of art. It was the culmination of a lifelong dream – to create large-scale sculptural work. He collaborated with the artist Carl Nesjar to create immense concrete casts of his sculptures and he later began to design more sculptures in steel and wire. Picasso had found himself classed as part of the artistic establishment by the new realist artists of the swinging sixties. And so, instead of resting on his laurels, he rebelled against both the existing and the emerging orthodoxies by developing new styles. The young rebel was only 82.

This angry struggle energised him for the next 10 years. In just seven months, in 1968, for instance, he crafted 347 etchings. By then he was 87 years old. In the last two years of his life, from age 89 to 91, he finished 201 paintings. These are glorious explosions of colour – savage celebrations of life, painted with *the power and lust-for-life of a mind that was alive, razor-sharp and angrily defiant of chronology and biology. On the 14th June 1970, at the age of 89, he painted 'l'aubade', which depicted an erotically-charged naked woman serenaded by a guitar-playing suitor. This was one of his last paintings.*

Now you can react to these stories in two ways: you can be inspired or you can be demoralised. If you feel demoralised, take a moment to think why. How old are you? Just turned 55? About to retire at 61? Maybe you are 47 but feeling gloomy about the sixth decade? Or perhaps you are 80?

If you felt demoralised by what Picasso did in his eighties, ask yourself why? When you think 50, 60, 70 or 80 – what comes to mind? Your mother or father? Perhaps they didn't live that long. Perhaps you have an image of someone plagued by ill health, living a restricted, limited life?

Or perhaps it was just their frame of mind – a closing of horizons, a limiting of experiences? Perhaps there was too little cash for new horizons, though such limitations are typically much more in the mind than in the world. Perhaps there was depression, a giving up.

But the relish and sharpness with which we live life (and to some extent the length of it) depends very much on whether or not we choose to act our age – or at least act some notion of how we are supposed to act at that age.

So, if you felt demoralised by Picasso's old-age vigour (he wasn't trapped by any 'venerable establishment artist' notion of how he should behave) this book is for you.

You don't want to stay sharp over 50? Fair enough, but you might want to study your own 'scripts' – your own preconceptions about what you should and should not do at your current age.

HOW CHALLENGE, CHANGE
AND LEARNING GROW THE BRAIN

In the 1920s and 1930s, Joseph Stalin forced millions of country peasants out of their farms into towns and cities, in one of the fastest, largest and most ruthless mass-movements of humanity in history. Millions died in the process, but tens of millions encountered a savage and dramatic change from quiet bucolic living to the noise and drama of industrial collectives, towns and cities. The great neuropsychologists Alexander Luria and Lev Vygotsky noticed something quite strange: they found that, as peasants moved from the country into the more complex cities, they became more intelligent – better able to solve complex problems, to reason and to think.

This increase in intelligence was almost certainly an extreme example of what has happened more gradually throughout the developed world over the last 90 years – the so-called 'Flynn Effect.' Named after the New Zealand sociologist James Flynn, who first identified it, the Flynn Effect refers to a progressive rise in intelligence in Western developed countries over the past century, as measured by standard verbal and nonverbal IQ tests. This rise may have levelled off over the past two decades, but a 30 year old in 1990 had, on average, a much larger vocabulary, significantly better verbal reasoning skills, and superior visual-spatial problem-solving abilities than an equivalent 30 year old in 1950.

Education and its sister – reading – offer the mental challenges to thinking, remembering and reasoning. This spreads connections between brain cells through the repeated stimulation of their high-level language and cognitive centres. During postmortem examinations neurologists have measured the connections between brain cells in the language areas of the left hemisphere. They found that the more education people had in their lives, the richer were the connections in the language areas of their brain.

This may be one reason why the more education and learning a person has had in life, the lower the risk that that person will succumb to dementia. What's more, research by scientist Robert S. Wilson and his colleagues in Chicago showed that nuns, monks and priests aged over 65 who were most mentally active – reading, doing crosswords and games, visiting museums and so on – had a roughly 50 per cent lower risk of developing Alzheimer's disease over a four and a half year period than those who were least mentally active[5].

Similar findings have emerged in animals: those that live in the animal equivalent of New York or London – with abundant stimulation, lots of neighbours and many mental challenges – have more densely connected brain cells and higher cognitive functions than those who live in relative solitude with comparatively little stimulation.

Challenge, change and learning: the ingredients of youth

Think back to when you were 20. Compare yourself then with how you are now. Don't compare obvious differences, such as body shape, physical fitness, hair colour, optimism and energy. Rather, compare only what your young and old self actually *did*.

Try to think specifically about three things – challenges, changes and learning. Let's start with challenge. Challenge here means the degree to which demands are made on you, or the degree to which you have to struggle for what you want.

Challenge isn't necessarily comfortable. What's more, you can be open to challenge but simply not *have* to fight for these things. The point of this questionnaire is to work out whether your present way of life makes the same level of demands on you compared to when you were in your twenties. Even if it doesn't at the moment, you can still create new and exciting challenges for yourself.

Your challenge quotient

Answer the following questions, comparing yourself now with when you were in your twenties:

Are you more challenged now by work/study?
Yes ☐ Maybe ☐ No ☐

Are you more challenged now by having to make money?
Yes ☐ Maybe ☐ No ☐

Are you more challenged now in being able to do the sort of things you really want to do? Yes ☐ Maybe ☐ No ☐

Are you more challenged now in maintaining close relationships?
Yes ☐ Maybe ☐ No ☐

Are you more challenged now in your efforts towards self-understanding and personal fulfilment?
Yes ☐ Maybe ☐ No ☐

Calculate your challenge score. Give yourself two points for every 'Yes', one for every 'Maybe' and nought for every 'No'.

💡 **7-10:** You find life more challenging now than in your twenties. This may be of your choosing or perhaps it has been forced on you by external circumstances such as job, relationship, financial or health changes. But whatever the reasons, life is challenging for you, and that means that you really need to try to have some of the mental sharpness you had as a 20 year old to cope with this.

💡 **4-6:** Life over 50 may be as challenging as life at 20 in some ways. Not all of this will be comfortable or even wanted. But positive challenge – and sometimes negative challenge too – can result in stimulating changes in your mind, brain and body. And to cope with this challenge, you really need to try to have some of the mental sharpness you had as a 20 year old.

💡 **0-3:** Like many of us who are over 50, your over-50 lifestyle has many fewer challenges than that of your 20-something self. Lack of challenge can be linked to contentment, but it can also be linked to a sense of boredom and life passing you by. There is a balance to be struck between the contentment and wisdom of maturity on the one hand, and the invigorating effects of challenge on the other. It is in meeting challenges, new people and ideas that we develop as individuals, and are forced to adapt and change. All of this, kept in proportion and without being overly stressful, can provide very healthy stimulation for both brain and body.

Your change quotient

Change is different from challenge. Challenge involves demands that you have to meet. Change, on the other hand, is optional. Change can be challenging, of course, and change which is forced on you is, by definition, a challenge.

When we are 20, change is the stuff of life: relationships, apartments, courses, hobbies, cities, beliefs, habits ... and so on. When we are 50, 60, 70 and older, the total amount of change in our life tends to decline.

Let's now compare the 20-year-old you with how you are now on this second ingredient of youth – change. Answer these questions:

Thinking of the next year, and comparing it with the year you turned 20, do you anticipate that in terms of work/career you will have:
> More change? ❏ No change? ❏ Less change? ❏

Thinking of the next year, and comparing it with the year you turned 20, do you anticipate that in terms of close relationships and friends, you will have:
> More change? ❏ No change? ❏ Less change? ❏

Thinking of the next year, and comparing it with the year you turned 20, do you anticipate that your leisure activities, social life and travel will have:
> More change? ❏ No change? ❏ Less change? ❏

Thinking of the next year, and comparing it with the year you turned 20, do you anticipate that the variety and range of un-familiar situations you will face will be:
> More? ❏ Same? ❏ Less? ❏

Thinking of the next year, and comparing it with the year you turned 20, do you anticipate that you will explore and open to change your philosophy of life and personal beliefs:
                    More? ☐ Neither more nor less? ☐ Less? ☐

Calculate your change score. Give yourself two points for every 'More', nought for every 'Less' and one point for any other answer.

7-10: Life is really changeable for you now, compared to when you were 20. This used to be unusual, but it is more common today, as divorce, redundancy and career change become more common. While this may well have its negative side for you, it is also an opportunity to maintain the mental youthfulness that change often brings. Change can also be stressful and throw up problems: you must be mentally sharp to cope with this.

4-6: You have some change in your life, albeit less than when you were younger. Change can be stimulating – but whether it is negative or positive, wished-for or not, you must develop your mental sharpness in order to make the most of it.

0-3: It is quite common for people over 50 to have a stable lifestyle that brings contentment and a welcome relief from the changes that often characterise earlier times of life. But the downside can be a sense of predictability and of 'being in a rut'. Habits can comfort, but they can also entrap. The feeling of being old follows close on the heels of such sentiments. You might want to bring a little more change into your life, because part of what makes young people young is the change they experience. You should work on your mental sharpness if you want to embrace these changes.

Your learning quotient

Let's now compare the 20-year-old you with how you are now by looking at the third ingredient of youth – learning. Answer these questions:

Thinking of the next year, and comparing it with the year you turned 20, do you anticipate that the amount of learning of new facts and skills that you will have to master will be:
More? ☐ The same? ☐ Less? ☐

Thinking of the next year, and comparing it with the year you turned 20, do you anticipate that the number of sports, hobbies or general interests that you will learn anew or systematically improve will be:
More? ☐ The same? ☐ Less? ☐

Thinking of the next year, and comparing it with the year you turned 20, do you anticipate that the amount of learning you will have to do to deal with different types of people from different backgrounds and outlooks will be:
More? ☐ The same? ☐ Less? ☐

Thinking of the next year, and comparing it with the year you turned 20, do you anticipate that the amount of learning about yourself as a person you will do will be:
More? ☐ The same? ☐ Less? ☐

Thinking of the next year, and comparing it with the year you turned 20, do you anticipate that the amount of learning about your family history, culture, community, country and/or politics that you will master will be:

More? ☐   The same? ☐   Less? ☐

Calculate your learning score. Give yourself two points for every 'More', one for every 'The Same', and nought for every 'Less'.

7-10: You are still learning a lot in a number of areas of your life. This is good, because part of what makes young people young is the fact that they are constantly learning. But learning demands at least some of the mental sharpness of youth and you may need to work at boosting your mental abilities.

4-6: You are still learning – which is good – but much less than when you were younger. Learning is a key ingredient of youth, and so everyone over 50 should keep on learning as much as possible. This requires mental sharpness, and you have to work at that.

0-3: 'Whew, I'm never going to sit an exam again,' is a fairly common response to leaving the school/college system and entering a career. These days, however, very few people find they no longer have to retrain and relearn, even if they manage to stay within one narrow career. In fact, if you are lucky enough to like what you do, and want to stay within a particular job/career, then new learning is probably essential to keep you competitive. And if you want to change career, or enter a career for the first time, after bringing up a family, for instance, then you must start learning the way most – though not all – 20-somethings have to do. This makes it essential that you tune up your mental capacities to be able to do this.

Three reasons to stay mentally sharp

There are three reasons why you should consider putting effort into staying mentally sharp. The first is so that you can rise to challenge, meet change and cope with learning as a younger lifestyle demands. The box, 'How challenge, change and learning grow the brain' (see page 25) explains the science behind this. The second is that mental sharpness helps you cope with stress. The third is that mental sharpness and mental activity can help combat some of the negative effects that ageing has on your brain and keep you more mentally fit as you get older. As a result, you can get more pleasure out of life and a better quality of life. Let's consider each reason in turn.

Reason one: To rise to challenge, meet change and cope with learning

You may not realise that you are not quite as mentally sharp as you once were until you have to cope with a new situation in life, learn a new skill or take on a new responsibility. Remember, most of us over fifties can draw on experience, cunning or delegation to get through our working lives: these don't need new learning.

If you scored between seven and 10 on each of the challenge, change and learning quotients, then your brain is certainly stimulated and – provided there is not too much stress involved – you are a long way towards achieving that 10-years-younger goal that we all should aim for.

You have a good reason to keep mentally fit – to make sure that you have the mental capacities to cope with the high levels of challenge, change and learning that you face.

If you scored three or less on any of the three quotients, then you should consider whether you are doing enough to achieve the 10-years-younger goal. Maybe you don't want to – that is fine. Plenty of people are very content to 'act their age', or at least act out conventional views of how one should be at that age.

But even if your work no longer challenges you, or you are no longer working and have little challenge in your social or leisure life, this does not mean that you have no reason to sharpen your brain to meet challenges.

Like it or not, when we are young, life throws up challenge after challenge – exams, friendships, sexual relations, career, finances. We master some of these and do less well at others. In fact, who we become as adults depends a lot on what challenges we master – our identity becomes tied up with this.

The sharper you are mentally, the easier it is to find new goals in your life, and to be creative about ways of achieving them.

Youth is a time of highs and lows, and we can all remember the highs – the exhilaration – of mastering a challenge, whether that be an exam passed, a job secured or a sexual relationship established.

Over 50, life tends to throw up fewer obvious challenges, although the challenges of the new prime of life can greatly exceed those of youth. But we can't just sit around and wait for life to produce them for us – we have to create them for ourselves.

Why? First, because there is nothing more exhilarating than mastering a challenge, all the more so if you are out of the habit. The feeling of success and control you get generates a host of very important chemicals in the brain and body, boosting immune function and enhancing brain function[6].

A second reason to create challenges for yourself is that rising to these challenges will boost your mental powers – cognitive as well as emotional. This, in turn, will change your perspective on the world, and with this changed perspective, you will see new opportunities and horizons that were invisible to you in your less sharpened mental state.

Some of these opportunities may be in leisure, others in your social life. You might also see opportunities for work – voluntary or paid, as employee or entrepreneur – as a result of sharpening your mental faculties by creating challenges for yourself.

You will also feel less daunted by the prospect of change in your life, and will feel better able to contemplate new learning which, in turn, can generate new opportunities.

Finally, the more you learn, the more you *can* learn. If you learn *how* to learn now, then you will find it easier to adapt, learn and change later on.

Reason two: Mental sharpness helps you cope with stress

Let me give you a practical example of how mental sharpness can help you cope with stressful challenges that life throws up. People of all ages differ in their degree of absent-mindedness. By absent-minded, I mean walking into a room and forgetting why you went in, starting one task and getting side-tracked into doing another, or keeping the wrapper and throwing the chocolate into the bin.

One study[7] looked at student nurses as they were about to undergo their first trial of real work in a range of different wards in a large, busy hospital. Some of these wards were high-stress workplaces, others were less stressful. The researchers measured the nurses' stress levels and also their absent-mindedness – an aspect of mental sharpness.

Of the nurses about to go into the high-stress wards, roughly half were quite absent-minded and half less so, but there was no difference in their personal stress level. The same was true of the other group who were going into the low-stress wards.

What was really interesting was what happened to these nurses six months later, at the end of a spell working in the wards. The mentally sharp, less absent-minded nurses showed no rise in their personal stress levels, irrespective of whether they worked in the low- or high-stress wards.

The absent-minded nurses who worked in the low-stress wards also showed no rise in their personal stress levels. It was a different story for the absent-minded nurses who worked in the high-stress wards, however. Their personal stress levels soared.

The high-stress wards posed a challenge that the sharper nurses could cope with because they were mentally more adept and not so easily overwhelmed by the demands made on them.

Although these were young people, the same principle applies to those of us aged over 50: we will cope much better with difficult challenges in our life if we develop mental sharpness. I'll show you later in the book how to become less absent-minded and hence better able to cope with the difficulties that life throws up.

 ## Reason three: To stay mentally fit and improve your quality of life as you age

There is growing evidence[8] that you may be able to combat some of the potential ravages of ageing on your brain late in life through continued mental activity.

For instance, one study in the Netherlands looked at several hundred people aged between 50 and 80 who had normal mental abilities. When they returned to study these people three years later, some of them showed signs of cognitive and memory problems. But the over-fifties who did mentally challenging work were much less likely to show these sorts of mental problems[9]. Many other studies have shown a strong link between ongoing mental activity and lower risk of age-related cognitive decline.

Mental sharpness is important, not only because it can help prevent the ravages of ageing, but – more positively – because it can enhance the quality of life at any age over 50. This is because of the extra opportunities that it opens up to people who stay mentally fit.

The earlier you start to consciously develop your mental sharpness, the more easily you will be able to stay mentally sharp as you get older.

Usually quite unconsciously, we gradually adjust our way

of life to what we feel our level of competence to be. You often see this in driving ability. Most people at some time in their 70s or 80s decide that it's time they avoided driving at night time, or in heavy traffic. This is a sensible adjustment of challenge to changed sensory and cognitive abilities.

The same happens for a whole range of tasks at all ages over 50. 'I couldn't face studying for that course – I'm just too out of practice.' Or, 'I could have faced that trip when I was younger, but not now.' Or, 'You know, I just can't be bothered with all the superficial chat involved in meeting strangers – I just like to be with old friends that I feel comfortable with.'

Some of these adjustments may make sense – reducing your risk of accident by driving more slowly, for instance – but others may limit you unnecessarily. This can result in a gradual reduction in opportunities for yourself without you even realizing that it is happening.

But these adjustments may be realistic from the point of view of your level of mental fitness. If you haven't used your memory much, then the prospect of organising a big trip and having to remember lots of things will indeed seem daunting.

If you have got out of the habit of concentrating and solving problems, then sorting out the financial and legal challenges of moving house or starting up a business may just seem too much for you to contemplate – even though part of you would like to try.

But it may be that you don't even contemplate such things because – unconsciously or not – you have limited yourself to a level of activity that you feel matches your mental abilities.

I am sure you can see the vicious cycle emerging from this.

Now look at the following chart. This shows how you can think yourself into a self-fulfilling spiral of think-old-behave-old. Believe me, your brain will respond to this: through having to cope with far less challenge, change and learning, physical changes will occur in your brain to reflect the lowered demands being made on it.

In this second step of this 10-years-younger programme, you have analysed to what extent your mental age is influenced by a lifestyle that does not include enough challenge, change or learning.

Even if you have enough of this type of youthful experience, however, you also have to consider the need to stay mentally sharp in order to cope with these demands.

In Step 3, let's consider some ways in which you might make your way of life richer in challenge, change and learning, and also at some of the potential obstacles to this.

Think old: avoid challenges and changes, don't learn

Lose confidence in being able to cope with challenges, change and learning

Limit the range of your activities and experiences

Less stimulation for your brain

Memory, concentration and problem-solving abilities reduced

Step 3:
Your Challenge Plan

'I've always wanted to ...'

The night Sean decided to give up his high-paying executive job to study medieval history at a major university, he felt a thrill of excitement mixed with intense anxiety. He had always regretted yielding to his father's pressure to train as a chartered accountant rather than going to university. In financial terms, his father had been right, but deep down Sean had never felt satisfied by his job, in spite of the high salary and stellar career progression that it had brought him.

Yet the challenges thrown up by this decision were huge: his family had grown used to his income and his wife had had to give up her career to look after the children because of the long hours and stresses of his job. How could the family function with Sean a full-time student? But at the age of 55, Sean felt he had to, for once, follow this deep-seated imperative rather than cold financial logic.

The challenges were not only financial: for his wife to take up her career again, he had to take over many of the home chores and duties. He found it frustrating that he couldn't pop into his local restaurant for a meal whenever he felt like it. He became easily irritated when some of his university teachers didn't deliver well-planned lectures. He found it hard to cope with the loss of status – just being one among hundreds of students.

Most of all, Sean found the deluge of reading and assignments he faced to be awesome. Used to a high-pressure environment and rapid-fire decision making, he found it very difficult to concentrate for the long hours that study required – and hard to take in all the new things he had to learn.

But all the stresses at home, in university and in his own mind slowly transformed into exhilarating challenges that made him feel decades younger.

Challenge areas of your life

If you have read this far, you clearly haven't rejected completely the notion that you should try to engineer your lifestyle a little in order to provide your brain with at least some of the stimulation that younger people are exposed to all of the time. You needn't go as far as Sean did, but challenge is an essential ingredient if you are to maximise your mental sharpness.

In Step 3 of the 10-years-younger programme, you may choose to ignore some of the areas as being of no interest to you. That is absolutely fine – skim over these, and concentrate on developing a programme tailored to your interests and needs. The important thing is that in at least one or two areas, you make a concentrated effort to increase the challenge, change and learning in this domain of your life.

The diagram below shows six broad areas of your life where you might consider increasing the challenge in your life to the level that young people have. Put a tick in any of these areas where: a) you feel that there are definite challenges for you – say, because of anxiety or lack of confidence, *and* b) you want to build challenge.

Challenge differs from change in that it involves doing something that seems difficult to you – where you feel that your personal, mental or emotional qualities aren't quite up to achieving it. For Sean, that was true from the moment he made the decision to change his life so dramatically. Change may be hard simply because any alteration in your life can be difficult or anxiety-provoking. However, unlike challenge, change itself doesn't involve these specific doubts about whether your resources can cope.

Let's now consider each of these six domains of challenge. Do try to work on at least a couple of them.

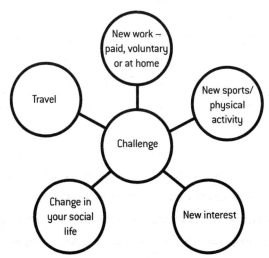

Work

Let's say that work is what you do to create both the means and the context for leisure. The human brain is designed to adjust to repetitive situations – we call this 'habituation'. If your life is 100 per cent leisure, then the word loses its meaning. This is because leisure is defined as 'restful or relaxing relief from the demands of work'.

If you are formally retired, you may or may not routinely do something that can be defined as work, but you may be kept busy and active with DIY, gardening, housekeeping and so on. If you are still in paid work, you might also do activities in your spare time that you classify as 'work'.

The critical definition of 'work' is that it is something you do for a purpose other than the pure enjoyment of the activity. That purpose can be to earn money, grow food, improve your house, contribute to society, or give pleasure to other people.

Clearly, for many people, work can give pleasure, and if you are formally retired, then the boundaries between work and leisure can become a little blurred. But enjoying your work does not take away from its definition as something you do for a purpose outside of yourself, and that is not *just* about enjoying yourself.

Another critical feature about work is our old friend *challenge*. This can be the challenge of problems to be solved, difficult people to be tackled, boredom to be overcome, effort expended, routine maintained, text written or organisations controlled. The box on the next page, 'Challenge, stress and work' explains why work challenge can be positive.

CHALLENGE, STRESS AND WORK

Challenge can have very important effects on your brain, and in particular on the availability of a key chemical messenger produced naturally in your brain – noradrenalin[10]. This is our very own 'wake-up' drug, but levels tend to reduce somewhat as people get older.

Noradrenalin is often linked to stress, and severe stress can result in something called hyper-vigilance – a state of anxious alertness that makes it hard to function properly. Some people who have suffered major trauma have difficulty sleeping and are jumpy at the slightest unexpected noise. Moderate levels of stress, however, can produce helpful injections of noradrenalin into your brain.

Stress arises when you feel required to do things that are beyond your abilities. Where that gap is too big, the stress can be unpleasant and unhelpful. Where that gap is more reasonable, however, then the resulting moderate stress – let's call it challenge – can be invigorating and motivating. What's more, it can be a spur to more effective learning.

Why does challenge improve learning? Challenge is a form of benign, moderate stress that increases levels of the chemical messenger noradrenalin into your brain. The noradrenalin released by challenge boosts the rate at which connections form between brain cells at the synapses.

As these 'synapses' are at the root of all learning, then it follows that challenge can boost brain power partly through 'oiling' the connections between brain cells. In other words, you are likely to learn better where you are benignly stressed by moderate challenge. Severe stress is quite another story that I'll return to later.

As I showed you earlier, people over 50 who are in mentally demanding jobs are much less likely to show a 'drop-off' in memory and other mental abilities[11]. One reason for this is that their brains are regularly being stretched – *challenged* – by mental demands that are non-routine and cannot be accomplished simply by falling back on well-practised habits.

What are the main work domains of your life?

How much does your work stretch and challenge your brain? First of all, think of those areas of your life that can be considered 'work'. You may have several – a paid job, the task of renovating part of your house, general housework, and membership of a community or political group. In the chart below, write in the main types of work domain in your life – if there is only one, that is fine.

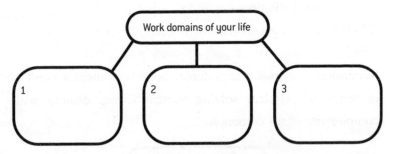

Work domains of your life

1

2

3

Rate your work challenge levels

Now take each of these work domains, and estimate the challenge level. Use a scale from nought to 100 where nought is totally unchallenging and 100 is excessively challenging to the point of being too stressful. The ideal score on this scale is 50 – challenging without being over-stressful. To help you fill this out, here are some examples of different scores:

0–10   Almost entirely unchallenging (though it may be enjoyable).

11–20   Occasionally a little challenging.

21–30   Moderately challenging some of the time.

31–40   Challenging quite a lot of the time.

41–50   About as challenging as it can be most of the time, but I can still cope.

51–60   A little too challenging at times.

61–70   Very demanding and challenging – quite stressful some of the time because the demands are a bit too much.

71–80   Highly challenging and definitely stressful a lot of the time.

81–90   Extremely stressful, too challenging, little respite from the pressure and demands.

91–100   I can't go on with this much longer!

Reminder: challenge means demands on your mental faculties in terms of problem solving, remembering, dealing with complex situations or people.

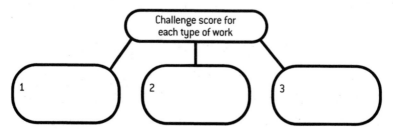

If your score was low (say, under 20) across all areas of work in your life, then you need to consider building more challenge into your work life, so as to give your brain more stimulation.

If your score was high (say, over 75) across all areas then you should consider whether you need to change these demands. Look at the section on stress (page 119) for advice.

You may have a mix of scores. For instance, your day job may be very unchallenging, but you may have a very stimulating role in a local organisation. It may be that it suits you very well to have one area of your work life that is nicely routine and undemanding – that's fine.

Looking at your scores, make the judgment whether you need to work on increasing the challenge in one or more areas of your work life. Tick the 'Yes' or 'No' box in the chart.

Boost your work challenge levels

If you ticked 'NO', then skip this section and go on to the sports/physical activity section (page 51).

If you ticked 'YES', consider how you might do this. Pick one area of your work life first. Here are some of the ways you can increase challenge:

☀ Increasing challenge in current work

Some jobs, by their very nature, are highly limited and restricted and it is hard to change the level of challenge they offer. For instance, if you collect tolls on a toll bridge, then there is relatively little you can do with this job to make it more challenging.

But many jobs have more flexibility, and most bosses welcome initiative from people in their organisation. In general, the principle 'You only get out of a job what you put into it' is true much of the time.

If you sit on a fund-raising committee, you may find that the personalities and organisation involved make this a dreary and unchallenging task.

But perhaps if you put a bit more of yourself – a bit more effort – into the committee, you might end up as chair. Then you would have more opportunity to raise the challenge levels by setting more ambitious goals, bringing in new thinking and so on.

Another way of making jobs more challenging is by doing additional training or reading around the subject. This will usually make the job more interesting and motivate you more.

Finally, depending on the organisation and the people in control, you might consider asking to be given a more challenging role.

If your work involves self-organised activities such as growing vegetables or renovating your house, you have much more opportunity to make the task more challenging. You can always increase the sophistication or complexity of what you are doing – for example, switching to organic gardening or renovating according to a particular period style.

Changing current work

Depending on your financial circumstances, on your training, and on the economic circumstances in your area, you might consider boosting challenge by changing your job. Unless you have thought about this already, this is something you should probably only consider once you have exhausted the possibilities of increasing the level of challenge in your current job.

If you are not in formal employment, then it is much easier to change your work to give yourself something more challenging to do. But again, it is probably best to try to change the challenge levels in your current work first.

Adding new work

If you are unchallenged in your current work life, there are endless possibilities for finding more challenging work. This may require some prioritisation and time management. You may even have to give up something you are currently doing. But it is well worth the effort.

Where to begin? Scan your local newspaper, get a brochure from your local schools and colleges, visit community centres and the local library. Make a list of as many different work activities as you can. Remember, voluntary work can sometimes turn into paid work, if that is important to you.

Build on your existing skills and experience, but consider developing new skills and abilities too (see Step 5: Your Learning Plan, page 79).

Set your challenge goals

Having read through the three sets of possibilities, set one, two or three goals for yourself that will increase the level of challenge in your work life. Write them down in the chart below.

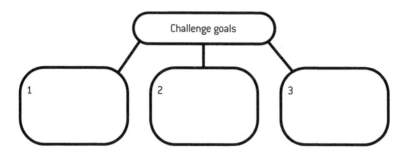

Sport/physical activity

Later in the programme, I'll tell you more about the positive effects of exercise on the brain. In this step, the focus is on challenge, however.

For some people who don't have much challenge in their work life, sport and exercise can be a major source of challenge.

Whether it is improving your technique in golf, increasing the number of lengths you swim in the local swimming pool or walking a route a little faster each day, these minor goals can stimulate your brain through both the challenge itself and the effects of the exercise.

If this is one of the challenge areas you decide to work on, complete up to three goals in the chart. Before you increase your level of physical activity significantly, seek your doctor's advice if you have been relatively inactive for a long time, or you have an ongoing medical condition, such as a heart or respiratory disorder or joint or spinal ailment. These conditions will not necessarily preclude exercise but you may have to adapt the type and level of activity you do.

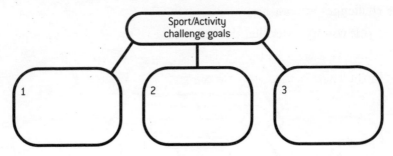

Interests

What do you do of a winter evening once the chores are done? Chat? Read? Watch television? Or do you have some indoor interest that absorbs you?

Most people of my age that I know seem to be too busy with the demands of work and family to have indoor interests. A few who play sport might read about the subject, but for a lot of people television is their only indoor leisure pursuit.

The problem with television is that it has been shown to leave you feeling lethargic after extended periods of viewing. That lethargy is the opposite of the effects that challenge can provide.

Of course, some programmes are challenging and stimulating, and I would always want to have a television set in the house. The problem is that you can so easily be seduced into watching television for long periods if you don't have other demands on your time.

As long as you have work and family commitments, then television can be a trouble-free relaxation zone where the lethargy of an evening's viewing can be a welcome break from the pressures of the day. But what about when work and family demands slacken off? Are you equipped to find new challenges in your life?

If you have decided that this is one of the areas of your life where you want to build challenge, make a note of the goals in the chart below.

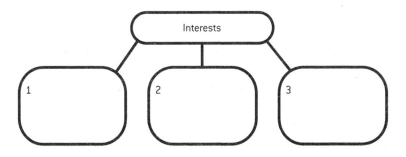

Social life

Social life is about pleasure, not challenge, you might think. Of course that's true, but ask yourself this question: do you sometimes find your social life a bit stale and predictable? If so, then you may need to broaden your social life a little – and this can be challenging.

Compare this stage of your life with your younger self: youth is about meeting new people, making new friends, exploring new relationships. It's also about trying out new activities and types of entertainment.

There are two broad aspects of social life, and these overlap with interests to a certain extent. These are meetings with other people and entertainment. Let's have a look at each of them in turn.

Meetings with other people

Human beings are highly social animals, and we were made to be part of a reasonably large social group. Interacting with other people may be very important in keeping our brain active and stimulated: the box, 'The social life of your brain' (page 56) explains why.

So how can we increase the challenge on our brains through more informal social meetings? In Mediterranean countries, a kind climate and the piazza make it so much easier for people to bump into each other informally, to chat and gossip. For those of us not fortunate enough to live in climates that allow us to mix informally every day with other people, we have to be creative in making sure that we find opportunities to mix casually with as wide a range of other people as possible. Colder climates tend to foster the developments of the club, bar or coffee house culture, but these are not to everyone's taste.

Some people are quite happy mixing with a small group of family and friends, and that is fine. If you are one of these, then you won't choose increasing informal relationships as one of your social goals.

Some people hate dinner parties, others love them. Some people grimace at the thought of coffee mornings, others thrive on them. Organised card games are anathema to some, bliss to others.

There are hundreds of possible formal or semi-formal ways that people concoct in order to meet with other people. You don't necessarily have to develop skills or buy equipment, but it could provide another learning challenge, for example, if you want to play bridge.

If you feel that you could do with more challenge in the area of formal or informal contacts with other people, make a note of a possible goal in the chart

☼ Entertainment

When did you last go to the cinema/theatre/concert? Include both amateur and professional performances. Write the approximate date in the chart.

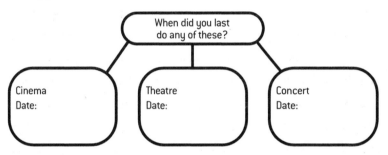

You may decide not to make entertainment your challenge goal for any number of reasons, including financial, availability or lack of interest. But before ruling it out, remember that there are many different forms of entertainment. For example, there is hardly a community in western civilisation that does not have amateur dramatic and music groups.

If you have decided to build challenge in this area, fill in your goals for the two areas of social life in the chart below.

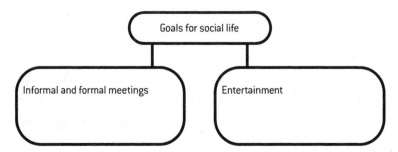

THE SOCIAL LIFE OF YOUR BRAIN

Animals that live in complex social environments have more developed brains and better mental functions than those that live in more isolated conditions. We are a highly social species, and for many people, mixing with others – particularly a challenging and changing range of others – can be of immense value in keeping the brain enriched and active. This enrichment both grows and strengthens the connections between brain cells as well as generating new cells in key memory areas of the brain.[12]

Socialising isn't to everyone's taste, and there are many different ways to stimulate your brain apart from meeting other people. What's more, the people you meet may not be very stimulating in themselves, and so there are circumstances where boosting your social life may not necessarily be the key to providing synapse-enriching stimulation.

So if you live on your own and can't or don't want to get out and about, don't worry: there are many different ways to stimulate your brain. But if you can, and are so inclined, the challenge of meeting other people can be one of the most effective ways of enriching your brain.

Travel

Travel is one area of your life where you can increase challenge, and it has the added benefit of allowing you to interact with more and different people.

Most people can think of some places they would like to go to but just haven't got round to, and other places that they would like to go to but don't feel up to the challenge of visiting just yet.

Some people would love to travel but can't because of financial, work or family limitations. Travel leaves some people cold.

Habit and routine can apply to travel as much as to anything else. It can be wonderfully relaxing to go to the same place for a holiday each year, but if the holiday has become stale, maybe you should think about changing the destination or changing what you do when you get there.

If you live on your own, and have the time and money, there are many fascinating small-group expeditions to almost anywhere in the world. These can range from the very civilised (studying Renaissance art in Tuscany) to the very remote (desert walking in Central Australia).

Whether on your own, or with a partner, close friend or relative, small group travel can be extremely challenging and stimulating. You will meet people you find difficult to get on with and people you really like. You will face taxing situations and exotic ones. The main thing is that it is unlikely to be stale and routine, and hence has a good chance of providing healthy stimulation for your mind and brain.

Travel need not involve great distances: it can be no further than neighbouring hills or mountains you have never climbed, or a nearby river you have never navigated.

If you decided to make travel one of your challenges, note down in the chart what your challenge goals for travel are.

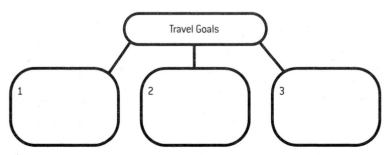

Step 4:
Your Change Plan

The morning train

As Marion squeezed into the train that morning and saw the same faces that she had seen for the last 15 years, she realised she was bored – no, more than bored – she was stale. Stale at home, stale at work and stale in the tennis club – her main social life. She remembered having that feeling before, when she was younger – funnily enough, it tended to come on as she travelled to work. In the past, when she had that feeling, she would immediately start looking for a new job, and she always got one, because she was good. But now, at 57, she wasn't going to risk her pension by leaving – especially as she might get an early retirement package in the next three or four years anyway.

Sitting in her usual seat, she found herself looking round at the other commuters in their usual seats. It occurred to her that they all seemed to dress in more or less the same clothes every

morning – and their hairstyles never seemed to change. At the
far end of the compartment she noticed Brian from the tennis
club – wearing the same design of rimless glasses that he had
worn since she first met him two decades before. Brian looked like
he and his tweed jacket had been dipped in amber and preserved
– apart from the steady loss of hair.

Her eyes drifted to the airfield that the train passed every
morning: a microlight aircraft was taking off, bouncing toy-like
in the wind. Marion's eyes followed it up into the sky, fixed on the
final speck before it peeled off south. A jolt went through Marion
– the same jolt she used to get each time she decided to change her
job. She looked down at the dark business suit she was wearing.
Today she would arrange an overdraft. On Saturday, she would
take this suit and all the other clothes in her wardrobe to the
charity shop and buy a completely new set of clothes – perhaps
with the aid of a personal shopping helper in a department store.
And she'd go to the optician and buy a new pair of glasses. Then
she'd get her hair done – short and sleek and trendy so it would
fit into the helmet. The helmet? It had come to her that she was
going to learn to fly a microlight.

Change can be challenging, but it is not the same as challenge. It is different insofar as habit and imagination, rather
than difficulty, are the main obstacles to change. Change can
also involve quite small, apparently trivial, areas of your life:
the breaking of routine can make you see things with fresh
eyes, and this is in itself stimulating because it makes you
attend.

ATTENTION

Raise your eyes from this book for a moment and pick something – an object, a colour, a shape – anything. For 30 seconds look at that object/shape/colour only. Don't just glance – fixate it as if you have never seen it before.

Now close your eyes and concentrate on the many sounds you can hear that you weren't aware of until now: the noise of cars, a voice, an electrical hum, a bird call. How many different sounds can you become aware of? Do this for 30 seconds.

Run your finger over a surface – any surface – such as a page of this book, the material of the chair you're sitting on, a wall. For 30 seconds, feel what it's like.

It is extraordinary what we see, hear and feel when we slip out of automatic pilot and *attend*. Being able to pay attention, to pick just one thing out of the millions of stimuli hitting our senses, is central to being conscious, to being self aware and, ultimately, to being human.

Attention is the gateway to many things, including learning. We are supposed to learn from new experiences such as travel or relationships, but we learn *nothing* from these things unless we *attend* to them. Remember, learning is about your brain being physically sculpted by experience: it is about the brain cells forming new connections because of the stimulation they receive from the outside world.

But we now know that these physical changes largely happen in response to the things we *pay attention* to[13]. This is why we can't learn when we are asleep: our brain responds to sounds and sensations, but because we do not attend to them, they do not embed themselves into the brain's web of connections: playing language tapes in your sleep won't work – any learning will only happen during brief periods of awakeness and that will be poor due to drowsiness.

This is also why some people can sail through life untouched by experience: their brains are only changed by experiences that they attend to. In busy lives, in self-preoccupied people, in stressed and worried people, attention to what is being experienced can too easily be lacking.

Of course, there are some occasions where it is *good* not to attend: it is best to distract yourself from painful dental or medical procedures and not attend to them. Not only is the pain lessened or avoided, but you do not learn to fear the procedures in the same way because you have not attended to them: they have not sculpted themselves into your brain.

Attended stimuli activate many more brain areas than do non-attended stimuli. Attention activates brain-enriching neuromodulators. These are brain chemicals that strengthen connections between brain cells. Attention is a critical ingredient for staying sharp. Our brains are programmed to attend to change, and so building a certain amount of change into your lifestyle will make you more attentive to your world, and hence keep you more stimulated. This, in turn, will give your brain much more rejuvenating stimulation than if you hurry through life without stopping to really *look*, *listen* and *feel*.

The chart opposite outlines different areas of your life. Put a tick in those circles representing areas that you think you could consider changing.

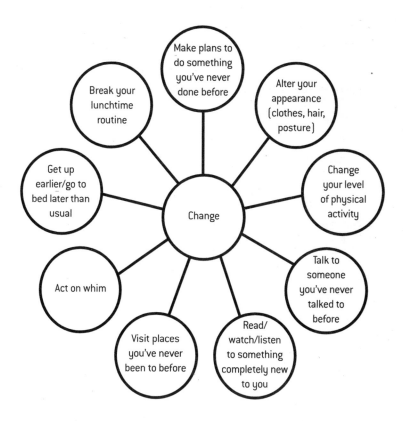

Areas for change

Change need not involve drastic alterations to your way of life. Change need only involve minor alterations in routine. One of the main reasons for making these changes is to force you to *attend*.

As you can read in the box on 'Attention and seeing' (page 65), most of the time we don't really *notice* what's in front of us – be it with our eyes, ears, nose, mouth or touch. Can you, for instance, think of an occasion when you drove along a stretch of road – maybe over many miles – and could not remember a thing about it?

When that happens, you are operating on automatic pilot: your brain can do a great deal without your conscious control or awareness. But it isn't just turning the steering wheel or pressing the pedals that are mindless habits – in this situation your eyes and ears are operating under automatic pilot also.

Have you noticed how time goes faster as you get older? One reason may be that less and less tends to change as we age. We have more and more well-established habits and routines. And as with driving for miles without awareness, so you can live for weeks and months with little conscious attention to what's going on around you.

Your very consciousness of the world can become a habit, and it is in the very nature of habits that they tend to dull conscious awareness. Habits allow you to do lots of things in your daily life that you could never possibly do if you had to consciously attend to them all.

When you are immersed in routine and habit, time inevitably goes faster. Routine has no need for attention, however, and your capacity to attend may dwindle through lack of practice.

This is why change is so important. Your brain can't help paying attention when something changes – it is one of the secrets of our survival as a species. And when you pay attention, you can't help becoming aware of the change: this in turn will slow down the passage of time.

Have you noticed how when you are on a holiday somewhere new, time seems to go much more slowly for the first day or two, and then speeds up inexorably until the end of the holiday? This is because of all the new sights and sounds and experiences the holiday brings: they force you to attend, and this slows down time.

1. Make plans to do something you've never done before

In the chart, write down three things you have never done that, over the next week or two, you can do. These can be very small things such as visiting somewhere near your home or work where you have never been before. Maybe you've never had a steam bath or a sauna. Have you ever had a manicure? A massage? There are literally thousands of small changes you can make that will cost you little or nothing in time or money. Write down three of them in the chart.

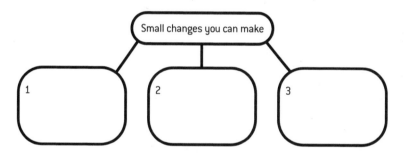

ATTENTION AND SEEING

Imagine the following scene. You're walking across the lobby of a big hotel when someone you don't know comes up and asks you for directions. While you're giving the directions, two men pass between you and the stranger, carrying a door. You think this is a bit rude, but they move on and you continue describing the way the stranger has to go.

When you've finished, he thanks you and then says 'You've just taken part in a psychology experiment. Did you notice anything different after the two men passed with the door? 'No,' you reply, puzzled. Then he tells you that he is not the man who originally asked for directions! That first man comes up to join you. You look at them side by side and see they are completely unalike – different height, complexion, hair colour, build and dressed differently! 'You're joking,' you say disbelievingly. 'No, we're not. One of us walked off behind the door and the other took his place.'

In this experiment led by Harvard psychologist Daniel Simons[14], roughly 50 per cent of those who took part didn't notice that in the course of a couple of seconds, the stranger they were talking to was replaced by someone who looked completely different. How can this be?

This 'change blindness' is another example of how we don't really 'see' the world around us much of the time. When the stranger comes up for directions, we tend to treat him as another *category* – here is a stranger and I have to work out how to tell him how to get to where he wants to go.

The key here is *attention*. We are attending to the instructions and not to the person. In fact, the person is irrelevant to the task in hand. What's more, in the jumble of experience that assails our eyes, we can't possibly take it all in. Hence our brains tend to 'fill in' this flotsam of background information by drawing on memory, stored images and experience.

But if we are projecting old stored categories onto the world rather than fully seeing what is in front of us, why don't we get knocked over by cars and buses, bump into tables, and ignore people we know when we see them in the street?

Well actually, people do all of these things from time to time, but for most of the time we manage to get around okay. This is because our brains are particularly sensitive to *changes* in scenes.

So, if a stranger you were talking to suddenly walked off and another replaced him, you would see their change of position and would have no trouble noticing the impostor. But because the change took place behind the door that two men were carrying, in at least half the cases studied the subjects didn't notice the switch.

Magicians are masters at using this 'change blindness'. If a card is quickly swapped while your eye is moving from one position to another, then your brain probably won't notice the change. In other words, for the fraction of a second that your eyes are moving, you are effectively blind. Clever use of distraction also plays a part in the ruse.

Why, then, don't we experience the world as a sequence of flickering images interspersed with periods of blindness? We don't because our brains 'fill in' the gaps and smooth out the world with remembered categories and rough sketches of experience.

There are other examples of this. The same Harvard researchers showed a group of people a video of a basketball game and asked them to count the number of passes made by one of the teams. A minute or so into the match, a man in a gorilla suit walked slowly across the court and in among the players. Though clearly visible for about five seconds, again only half the viewers noticed him.

Watching the same game again, but without carrying out the task of counting passes, the same group saw the gorilla easily – and found it hard to believe that this was the same video they had watched a few moments before!

Again, this shows that we miss much – indeed most – of what is in front of our eyes, ears and other senses. Making little changes in our lives can help us to attend to much more, and hence gives our brains much more enriching stimulation than they would otherwise receive.

2. Alter your appearance

When a young police officer puts on a uniform for the first time, it almost certainly feels strange and foreign. Yet other people react to that uniform in a range of more or less predictable ways – just as they do to a priest or to a white-coated doctor.

These reactions help to make the police officer feel a part of the uniform and more comfortable with the role that goes with it. This is the point of uniforms: they help people think themselves into a particular way of behaving, and communicate clearly to other people what function that person is expected to perform.

Our dress and appearance are a sort of uniform as well, whether we like it or not. They are very powerful statements to other people about what to expect from us. Equally, they are powerful statements to ourselves about what to expect of ourselves. This, together with the way other people react to our appearance, powerfully shapes how we feel, think and behave. The chart below shows this cycle.

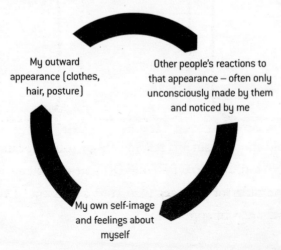

My outward appearance (clothes, hair, posture)

Other people's reactions to that appearance – often only unconsciously made by them and noticed by me

My own self-image and feelings about myself

Put yourself in the shoes of someone you are only slightly acquainted with. That person has been asked by someone – employer, bank, credit agency, intelligence group – to describe your appearance and carry out a preliminary assessment of you as a person on this basis alone. As they do not know you well, they have to rely solely on your appearance and not on some deeper knowledge of you as a person.

In the chart below, write a brief description from this acquaintance's point of view. In particular, what might this person say about your age? Write this separately for the three main aspects of appearance – clothes, hair (include facial hair) and posture. Try to write as dispassionately and objectively as possible. Remember, this person scarcely knows you, and is not a mind reader. He or she cannot therefore know anything about the youthful thoughts, behaviours and propensities you might have other than is revealed by your appearance.

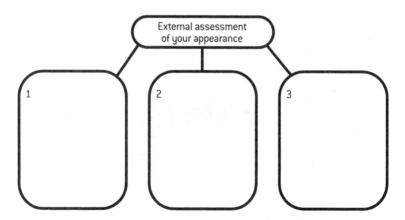

What did the assessments tell you about your appearance? Do you have a disdain for fashion? Do you convey an image of someone older or younger than your actual age? Let's cover the three areas of appearance.

☀ Clothes

Fashion is fickle and can also be expensive. Some people are rather obsessed with keeping up with it, while others are contemptuously dismissive of it. Plenty of mentally youthful people ignore fashion. You may or may not choose to include the way you dress as one of your change goals.

On the other hand, paying even token homage to current fashion does signal something quite important to people – that you are someone who is open to change, and who is responsive to the contemporary world. This makes it harder for people to pigeon-hole you as an 'old fogey'.

In a competitive work situation, for instance, dressing fashionably can be a defence against younger colleagues who perhaps have an interest in portraying you as someone who is out of touch. Showing some sensitivity to fashion – trivial and apparently wasteful as it may be – may help confound the stereotypical impression that grey hair and wrinkles can arouse.

For stereotypes about age, remember, are not just a problem in *your* mind: they are even more of a problem in the minds of other people, particularly younger ones. And as you saw above, other people's reactions – albeit often subconscious – have an enormous effect on your own self-image and hence on your own mental age.

If you need further persuasion, remember the research I told you about earlier, that just reading age-related words slowed down the walking speed of people of all ages. Remember, these people *were completely unaware* of the change in their walking speed.

Hair

What can be more quintessentially emblematic of your age than the colour, shape and quantity of your hair? The multi-billion pound market in hair products worldwide is evidence of this.

One interesting trend among balding men of all ages is to shave their heads completely. This can be a rather trendy thing to do depending on the social milieu. This is one way of escaping from the stigma of hair loss – abolishing hair and therefore declaring it irrelevant.

So, sir, maybe that frazzled semi-circle around its wispy companions on your bald head would be better completely removed? Or maybe it would be worth asking for some more expensive hairdressing advice as to how to present yourself above the eyes?

Hair dye isn't necessarily the answer either, but consider this: politicians of both sexes spend enormous amounts of time and money fretting over their appearance. Why? Because the public's perception of them is heavily influenced by such superficialities.

Remember, appearance is important because it influences how other people respond to you, which in turn influences how you respond to yourself. Your hair (or lack of it) is an extremely important part of that appearance.

Posture

Have you begun to stoop a little as you walk? This isn't only a feature of age, but ask any child to mimic an older person, and they will probably hunch their shoulders and bend their back.

Of course there can be good physiological reasons for these changes in posture, but equally often it is a habit of carriage that is linked to feeling and thinking old. It has been shown that we quite unconsciously pick up a posture simply by being beside people who adopt that posture. If we spend a lot of time with people who have old-type postures, then it is very likely we will pick them up also.

Assuming that there is no medical reason for your stoop or rounded shoulders, you might like to think about changing this aspect of your 'behaving old' repertoire. Some people find that yoga or the Alexander Technique are helpful in improving their posture. Others just catch a glimpse of themselves in a shop window and pull their shoulders back.

If you feel like it, have a look at recent photographs of yourself, and compare them with photos of you 20 years ago. Can you see any difference in posture? Even though there are physical changes in our bones, muscles and joints that are caused by age, your mental age may have a big impact on how much these actually affect your posture.

You might care to take a look at yourself side-on in a mirror. Can you detect any changes in your stance that might be evidence of your mentally succumbing to some conscious or unconscious view of yourself as old?

I've already shown you how your speed of walking is linked to unconsciously-perceived ideas about age. We can all think of people in their seventies and eighties who have a sprightliness in their walk that reveals a youthful self-image.

What about walking? How would someone describe you as you walked down the street? Do you exude a positive, active, optimistic view of life in your posture and style of walking?

Okay, so you are not necessarily active and optimistic. But remember the artificial smile that boosts mood? So it is with other manifestations of outlook. If we behave *as if* we are youthful, active and positive, then we have a much better chance of beginning to *feel* these things.

Which brings us on to another aspect of change – physical activity.

3. Change your level of physical activity

Whether or not you decide to make sport/physical activity part of your challenge goals, it's worth considering whether you can introduce change in your life by altering the type or level of physical activity you engage in.

Physical activity isn't really an option if you want to stay mentally young. As you'll see in the later steps, physical fitness is possibly the single most important factor in helping your brain to stay young and fit.

But even without upping the level of your current activity, you might want to consider trying out some different types – swimming, running, gym, tennis, for example. Or maybe you can simply walk to places that you normally drive to, or change the route or time of your jog.

4. Talk to someone you've never talked to before

One very important difference between young and old people is the number of new people they meet and talk to every year. Young people congregate in great changing groups in school, college, night clubs, parties and other places. The older you are, the fewer people you tend to mix with.

People are about the most powerful stimulus that you can have. However, when you get older you tend to mix with a smaller group of people and encounter less novelty in other human beings. There are, of course, exceptions to this, but in general this holds true.

So, for some of us at least, our mental ageing might be exaggerated because we get far less stimulation from meeting new people.

In any one day, you probably see many people that are familiar to you but whom you may never have spoken to. Maybe you have gone into the same shop for 30 years and never had a conversation with the shopkeeper. Perhaps there is a colleague at work whom you have never exchanged more than the odd hello with.

This kind of change can be much easier when you have set some challenges linked to new activities, interests or sports – as I discussed in the challenge section earlier. But even without changing your routine, you might be surprised by the stimulation of trying to interact a bit more with a greater range of people around you.

5. Read/watch/listen to something completely new to you

Have a look in your local newspaper or entertainment guide. Call in at your local book shop and music shop. Resist the temptation to go for the familiar. Hate ballet? Go to a performance. Loathe modern art? Visit the travelling exhibition you saw advertised. Bored by poetry? Buy the best-selling book of verse. Find politics unbearably tedious? Make an appointment to see your local councillor or parliamentary representative about an issue that is of concern to you. Or buy/rent a video or DVD of some political biography or documentary. Love classical music? Don't buy it! Try some of that rap music that you detest instead. Hate soccer? Go to a soccer match.

The important thing is to start behaving more the way younger people behave. They tend to experiment with a range of different types of entertainment, books and music. You did too when you were younger, but then you found what you liked and stuck with it, probably.

People change, however. In fact, everything changes. We should try to keep our minds open to different types of culture and entertainment so that we can discover likes and even loves that we rejected or never sampled earlier in life.

The more we do that, the more stimulated we will feel, and the less time will seem to race by in a blur of habit and familiarity.

6. Visit places you've never been to before

Most of us live within a small familiar subset of our locality. We tend to follow the same routes, and go to the same places. Most of us do not *explore*. It may be that one suburban street is much like another, and that one office block is surrounded by much the same parking spaces as any other.

But you might be surprised. It may only take an extra five minutes on your way home, but why not explore that road or path you've passed so often, but never been down before? Who knows, you might see something that will be of use or interest to you.

Have a look at a map of your locality? Have you ever been to that deprived estate, to that millionaire's row, to that funny-shaped park in an unfashionable area of town?

Maybe you'll be more adventurous and go somewhere 50 miles away that you have never been to before. Or perhaps you will get on a plane and fly to a city you have never visited before.

The point is to keep your curiosity exercised, and thus your mind stimulated. It is about breaking habits of action and perception. It is about seeing things for the first time. That, after all, is one of the hallmarks of youth – everything being so new.

There is far more in the world that you have never seen than you have seen. But we think ourselves into narrow alleyways of habit where everything is familiar.

7. Act on whim

I've been asking you to plan a lot. You have to plan if you're going to change ingrained habits. But sometimes you should tear up plans. Do something completely on whim. If not now, then tonight, tomorrow morning, or this Saturday. Do something that would make your friends or family surprised.

If you can't think of something, pick up a newspaper, magazine or book. Look randomly through it and let your mind roam through the millions of associations stored in your memory. Pick a routine or habit and break it – just this once.

8. Get up earlier/go to bed later than usual

You've got nothing important on tomorrow? Get up at 4am tomorrow. Alternatively, stay up until 4am. Just occasionally, see how the world outside your house looks at times that you don't usually see it. It's amazing how different places can be at an early or a late hour. You notice people that you don't see at your normal times. You notice animals that you don't normally see. Places are changed. Try it.

9. Break your lunchtime routine

Don't eat lunch tomorrow. See if you can doze for 15 minutes. Or go for a walk, or run, or swim. Or walk to somewhere new. Or lie down somewhere and listen to a piece of music. Or go to a shop, museum, park, concert, church, temple, mosque instead of your usual lunch spot.

Or just sit in silence, trying to identify all the different noises around you that your brain normally screens out.

Do anything you like at lunchtime tomorrow, except what you usually do.

Step 5:
Your Learning Plan

A confession

Okay, I'll come clean. A white-haired 50-something professor, I am surrounded by young and clever postgraduates and fellows. It pains me to say this, but I am also a bit lazy. A new technology comes along – say a complex new statistical software package. Do I roll up my sleeves and bend my brain to the complexities of it? I'm afraid, I don't: I pick a couple of these clever young brains and get them to learn it. They do the learning and I sit back and benefit from the technology.

It's a common pattern: the older you get, the more you tend to end up managing other people rather than doing the work yourself. There are exceptions to this – some barristers and court judges for instance, who have to use their raw brainpower to take in a lot of information, often in new areas that they are not familiar with.

So, how much of the poor memory and loss of mental sharpness that hits the over-fifties happens because we sit back and let others do the learning? With varying mixtures of experience and low cunning, we get others to use their brains, while we rest on the laurels of accumulated experience.

The thing about experience, however, is that deploying it does not challenge and stimulate our brains nearly as much as learning new information: it's the equivalent of taking the lift to the third floor rather than walking.

Like your leg muscles – if you don't use your brain, it gets 'flabby'. Some of the lack of sharpness of age is just the flabbiness of under-use, and not the sign of an inevitable loss of brain cells.

LEARNING AND YOUR BRAIN

Earlier on you read an astonishing fact: the more education you have in your life, the more densely connected are the brain cells likely to be in at least one region of your brain – the left hemisphere language areas. Your risk of being diagnosed with Alzheimer's disease in later life is also lower, the more education and learning you have undertaken in your life (though of course many highly educated people succumb to Alzheimer's disease and many non-educated people do not – this is about *risk and probability*). This makes sense when you realise that learning not only stimulates new connections between brain cells – but also the *growth* of *new* cells[15]. We also know that people who use their brains a lot in their work later in life show better mental functioning than those who do not. In short: learning, together with its sisters challenge and change, literally grow your brain – that's why they are essential ingredients for staying sharp when over 50.

Boost your learning

Learning is what defines youth. We spend much of the first 20 years of our lives in institutions specifically built to make us learn. Learning, above all other mental activities, physically changes our brains.

The box opposite, 'Learning and your brain', explains how new learning not only builds connections between brain cells, but probably also generates new brain cells. It also explains how the total number of years of learning you undertake is strongly linked to your risk of dementia in later life.

The chart below shows a wide range of areas that can boost your learning. Tick those you might consider, then go

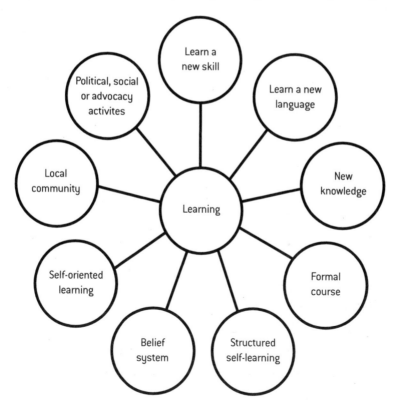

back and add or subtract from these areas once you have read them (below).

1. Learn a new skill

When did you last learn a new skill? You learnt to read in your first decade, to swim, ride a bike or drive in your second decade. You may have learnt the tools of your trade, if you have one, in your third decade.

But what about your fourth, fifth, sixth, seventh and eighth decades? How many new skills have you learnt?

In the following table, you can see the decades of your life listed along the top, and various skills listed down the side. There are also some empty spaces for you to fill in with skills specific to you that I have not included.

Put a tick under the decade that you learnt each skill. When you have done that, count up the total number of ticks for each decade.

The vast majority of people have many more ticks in their first three decades than in subsequent decades. Is this true for you? If not, congratulations. It's not easy to keep the brain young and stimulated by learning new skills.

This is because we are not usually made to do it. It's pretty normal to be learning a new skill when you are 20. Most of your friends will be in the same position. If you're 60, it's much less common. This means that those of us in an older age group have to be self-starters and not rely on the trends around us.

As you saw in the box on learning, acquiring new information is a powerful drug that revives cells, connections and

	0–10	11–20	21–30	31–40	41–50	51–60	61–70	71–80
Reading								
Writing								
Swimming								
Riding bike								
Driving								
Sport 1								
Sport 2								
Computer								
Foreign language								
Musical instrument								
Typing								
Cooking								
Work skill 1								
Work skill 2								
TOTAL NEW SKILLS LEARNED								

chemical messengers in your brain. One reason that we are less sharp when we are over 50 is that we simply don't bother learning as much as we did when we were young.

So, if you have decided to make a new skill one of your learning goals, what's it going to be? Jot down as many ideas as you can in each of the categories in the chart. Brainstorm – don't think about whether you'd like to acquire them or not, or whether they are feasible for other reasons. Just scribble down as many possibilities under each category.

There are literally thousands of possibilities, ranging from calligraphy to welding, book-keeping to yoga, meteorology to flower arranging, bonsai gardening to astronomy, digital photography to golf. You can choose to try a few different ones, or really go in-depth into just one.

Now do this:

- ·Q· Go back to the chart above and circle a few of the possible learning areas that you jotted down.
- ·Q· Choose one of these skills.
- ·Q· Next, create a plan as to how to set about learning the skill. You may be interested in learning to sail a boat or become a sushi cook, but haven't a clue how to set about it.
- ·Q· The biggest step you can take is to do something specific right now, or as soon as possible, to advance – even by a very small amount – your plan to learn a new skill.
- ·Q· If you have an Internet connection, log on and search for entries on your chosen area in your locality. If you don't, go to your local library or Internet café. If you don't know how to use the Internet, you might consider making this your first skill to learn.

Skill	Tick	Skill	Tick
Computer:		**DIY:**	
Word processing		Woodwork	
Desk-top publishing		Plumbing	
Page design		Electrical repairs	
Internet research		Plastering	
Web design		Bricklaying	
Digital pictures			
		Leisure:	
Business:		Wine-tasting	
Book-keeping		Genealogy	
Management		Bird-watching	
Public speaking		Amateur dramatics	
Writing reports			
		Cookery:	
Arts and crafts:		Cake making	
Calligraphy		Cordon bleu	
Watercolours		Sushi	
Oil painting		Entertaining	
Figure painting			
Still life		**Gardening**	
Sculpture		Hot house plants	
Pottery		Cacti and succulents	
Flower arranging		Fruit and vegetables	
Dressmaking		Garden design	
Lace making			
		Sport	
General interest:		Golf	
History		Bowls	
Literature		Tennis	
Economics		Badminton	
Biology		Horse riding	
		Sailing	
		Canoeing	
		Rambling	
		Climbing	

In fact, if you are over 80, and don't know how to use the Internet, I strongly advise you to learn: the Internet can be an enormously liberating connection to the whole world, particularly if you have limited mobility.

But you don't have to use the Internet to find out about your new skill. Your local newspaper, community centre, college, school, church, temple, mosque, sports centre or council will be sources of information. Remember, don't waste time wondering if you could or should: *just do it!*

But in learning your new skill, whatever it is, remember the issues of self-belief and motivation. If it is 30 years since you learned a new skill, then it will seem much harder to learn it now. This isn't because 'You're too old' – it's because you're out of practice. You have to *learn how to learn* again.

2. Learn a new language

Learning a new language isn't for everyone. It is a special type of skill that, if you have any inclination for it at all, can really make nourishing demands on your brain.

As you can see in the box opposite, 'Learning a second language and your brain', people who are bilingual have enhanced mental abilities in general and particularly in the areas of attention and mental control, and not just in language.

We don't know specifically that learning a small amount of Spanish or Italian will have these effects, but we do know that learning has very positive general effects on the brain.

Also, learning a language often requires interaction with other people and sometimes travel. These can be immensely stimulating in themselves.

LEARNING A SECOND LANGUAGE AND YOUR BRAIN

If you speak two languages fluently, your brain has to switch tracks continuously: it is mentally demanding because the brain has to shut down – inhibit – the language you are speaking currently and switch into the second language. This happens mostly in the frontal lobes – the brain's mind manager – as you'll see later.

The frontal lobes are the part of the brain most likely to shrink with age. But in older people who are bilingual, this ability to switch from one stream of thought to another is much more intact than in people of the same age who are not bilingual[16]. This is not only true when it comes to the two languages – it is *generally* true. In other words, as a result of the stimulation and training of constantly switching between two languages, they have improved their general mental sharpness.

Learning a second language later in life may not necessarily have this effect, but we know that learning in general has positive effects on the brain. If you really practise your new language, it is a pretty fair bet that you will improve not only your learning capacity, but also a number of other key mental functions that are central to staying sharp.

3. New knowledge

Learning a new skill almost always involves acquiring new knowledge as well. And you retain knowledge best by *doing* rather than acquiring it in a purely abstract form.

If your passion is a subject such as history, you could visit sites of historical interest. Perhaps you could join a local

historical or archaeological group and help out with a reno-
vation project or an excavation.

If your interest is the environment, for instance, you could
take part in a conservation or campaigning group on the natural
environment. Or you may prefer to build up your knowledge in
the comfort of your own home. As you will see when we come
to memory later in the programme, you should try to build your
knowledge using as wide a range of materials as possible.

Don't just rely on one medium such as books. Use videos,
DVDs, pictures or audio recordings dealing with your area of
interest. See if you can find some particular local dimension to
the subject you are interested in. If you are inclined to use the
Internet, I guarantee there will be scores, if not hundreds, of
sites and discussion groups with relevant information.

Try to meet people who are also interested in your subject
area, whether on the Internet, chatting to enthusiasts on the
other side of the world, or through local connections.

Even if you don't yet have a fully developed interest, and
are only toying with the idea, remember that interests grow
by learning, and don't exist ready-formed, to be discovered.

You can also consider doing a formal course, whether face
to face, distance learning, or via a computerised or Internet-
delivered package. This is what I'll consider briefly now.

4. Formal course

You spent a significant chunk of your life learning in formal
educational institutions such as school and perhaps college.
Many jobs these days require people to go on formal courses
to learn about new techniques, regulations and procedures.

Medicine, clinical psychology and most other professions now have a requirement that to continue practising in the profession, you are obliged to engage in on-going professional development. In some areas – information technology for instance – the changes are continuous and so rapid that many jobs in these areas are almost defined by the need to be constantly learning.

But many millions of working people continue to draw on experience, guile and a formal education that are now 20, 30 or 40 years out of date. This is probably not the best situation for their long term employability or for their mental well-being.

Perhaps you are not in formal employment and have no need or desire to be. For you it is even more important to keep your brain stimulated through new learning. Joining a formal course can be one of the easiest ways to get back into learning.

This is because that is how most people have learned in the past. The structure of the course, expectations of the teacher, and company of other students impose a discipline and motivation that can be difficult to achieve when learning on your own.

Most educational institutions run adjunct courses. Take a look at what's available in your local colleges and schools. You might consider studying for a formal qualification. In Britain for instance, the Open University is a fantastic institution that offers high-quality education through a mixture of distance learning, group tutorials and residential schools.

Mental exercise is as important as physical exercise. 'What are you studying?' shouldn't just be the conversational gambit of 19 year olds – it should be a standard question posed to everyone over 50. So, what are *you* studying?

5. Structured self-learning

You don't have to choose between formal courses on the one hand, and completely self-taught learning on the other. This book is an example of a structured programme that you can work through. But there are many other ways of teaching yourself a skill or body of knowledge.

E-learning helps you work through a domain of knowledge, often using computer or Internet technology. Learning a foreign language, for instance, can be made hugely easier if you buy commercially-available CDs or audio tapes where you can not only hear phrases spoken in the language, but which repeat themselves so that you can correct your responses.

There is a growing number of structured programmes that you can use to help give some shape and support to your learning, rather than leaving it all to your own direction.

6. Belief system

Do you have a belief system such as Judeo-Christian, Buddhist, Muslim, Humanist or some other? Maybe you are an atheist, or an agnostic. Perhaps you don't think about this and have no need for a specific belief system.

The point here is not what you believe but that your belief system – or the search for a belief system if you don't have one – can be an opportunity for learning.

It is common for people in their teens and twenties to try to work out their place in the world, and to experiment with different faiths and belief systems. This is all part of the learning nourishment of the young brain.

As we get older, this kind of trial and error experimentation becomes lost in a 'been there, done that' frame of mind. We tend to hold onto our beliefs – or lack of them – based on conclusions we came to during a period of questioning and experimentation maybe 30 years earlier.

Our beliefs, in other words, can become mindless habits just like any other aspect of our behaviour.

This is not for everyone, clearly, but if you are so inclined, you might choose to use your belief system as a basis for learning. You could learn more about your current set of beliefs, or about some other set that you don't adhere to.

7. Self-oriented learning

Learning more about yourself is a close companion to learning more about your belief system. I don't want to encourage fruitless navel-gazing or undesired self-exploration, but some people find it helpful and stimulating to explore their own thoughts, emotions and propensities, for example, through meditation, retreats or group discussions. There are also a wide range of self-help manuals aimed at self-exploration.

Change makes such self-examination inevitable. If we don't re-evaluate our priorities, relationships and behaviour periodically, we tend to run into trouble. Just ask any workaholic whose marriage has collapsed.

Change is an absolute given in life, and part of both the joy and the stress of being in your teens and early twenties comes from adapting to an environment that is much more changeable than it tends to be later in life. The joy and stress come not just from change *per se* – but also from the information these changes reveal about you as a person. Most changes chip away at that person, moulding them gradually, or sometimes dramatically.

Getting older brings with it its own raft of changes to your body, your relationships, your work and your social life. Our self-image is bound up with these areas of life, to a greater or lesser extent.

John's self-image may be strongly linked to his physical appearance and performance, which makes changes in these domains a major challenge to his view of himself. Charlotte might be so identified with her work role that when she loses her job or suffers a demotion, her whole sense of self is threatened. Kate might be at a complete loss when her children leave home.

Most of us negotiate these inevitable changes to our self-image in a semi-conscious way. A mixture of daydreams, dreams, night-time ruminations and – maybe – conversations, help us negotiate new agreements between our changing world and our changing selves.

But some of us manage this better than others. Men are less likely to discuss how they feel with other men. They tend to talk more about things outside themselves, and don't have the same degree of confiding, intimate relationships that women do.

But everyone is in the same boat – like it or not, they are having to learn new things about themselves, and they have to learn to think, feel and behave in different ways.

In other words a bit of self-reflection is essential for all of us from time to time. For many, this is second nature and is something you do with friends or with yourself. For others, though, some structured help with this self-reflection can be useful.

Self-help books, tapes and computer programs are one way. This book is an example of the genre, but with a particular focus on mental sharpness rather than on more general self-examination.

Groups – whether face to face or over the Internet – can be another way of helping in this adaptation to change. There are literally thousands of places where you can meet other people in similar situations, but of course many of them may not be to your taste.

I am not necessarily talking about psychological therapy. If you feel in need of therapy, it is for you to decide, perhaps in consultation with your doctor. Psychological therapy can be very helpful, but for the majority of people it is not necessary.

However, in order to adapt to inevitable change, a certain amount of self-reflection is necessary. How you do that will be a highly individual matter for you. For some of you, however, this might be an opportunity for learning that could be both simulating and invigorating.

8. Local community

How much do you know about your own locality? Do you know what's going on? Do you know who the local leaders/representatives are? Are you familiar with the issues facing your locality?

Learning about your local community – and participating in it – can be a potentially important way of adapting to change and hence aiding learning.

If you would like to make this one of your learning areas, take some time to study your local newspapers or Internet sites. Go along to meetings. Speak to people who are active locally. Interacting with other human beings can be the most potent form of learning.

9. Political, social or advocacy activities

Following on closely from the subject of your local community is that of political activity – local or national. Spreading out from this there is an enormous range of single-issue, campaign and charitable activities that involve many millions of people worldwide.

You may not be a political person. Indeed, learning about current politics may strike you as a waste of time. But it is likely that you are concerned about some wider social issues, whether it be the environment, heritage, crime, consumer affairs, housing, health or any one of hundreds of other subjects.

If you are, you might consider joining a group – either face to face or over the Internet – working on the issue that concerns you. This will be an excellent opportunity for learning.

Finding the time

You may be thinking to yourself, 'I would love to learn, but I just don't have the time.' It's amazing how things expand to fill the available time: this fact of modern life is a big obstacle to bringing change and new activities such as learning into your life.

But the truth is that most of us don't manage our time very well: we tend to fritter it away on relatively unimportant things, leaving little for more important – and, particularly, new – activities. Given that novelty and change are key parts of staying sharp, not managing your time well is a key obstacle to your stay sharp programme.

Learning is important – you should make time for it. In the chart below, fill out your activities during a typical weekday, and then do the same for a typical Saturday and Sunday. Sort your activities into three columns: very important; medium importance; low importance.

Activity	Very Important	Medium Importance	Low Importance
Early am			
Late am			
Early pm			
Late pm			
Early evening			
Late evening			

For instance, if you spend a lot of time reading emails or on the Internet first thing in the morning, put that in under the three columns opposite 'early am'. If email and Internet are very important to you put 'email' into that column. If it is less important, put it into one of the others. Now pinpoint a slot in your day where you are doing a less important activity and slot in 'learning' there. Now do the same for a Saturday and a Sunday.

Step 6: Can You Change?

Sam's Dad

When Sam hit 60, all he could think about was his Dad. His father left the company he had worked for after 36 years and moved into the armchair where he spent most of the next 11 years until he died. Sam remembered trying to persuade his father to go out and try new things, meet new people – anything but sit in front of that damned television. 'You can't teach an old dog new tricks,' was how his Dad always responded to Sam's urging, the ghostly images of daytime television flickering across his father's face in the winter-darkened living room.

Now Sam was 60 and suddenly free. Well, that was how it was supposed to be – but he didn't feel free. Like his father, he had been a bit of a workaholic. Like his father, he hadn't developed many interests because he put so much into his work. Like his father, he had found himself in retirement at 60. And now, as he contemplated what to do with the next few decades of his life, Sam felt weighed down with his father's pessimism. A friend dropped in one day: he looked at Sam and said 'This isn't a rehearsal Sam – you can't spend the rest of your life sitting here.' The comment sent a jolt through him. He realised that the 20 or 30 years ahead of him were under the control of just one person – himself. Sam shook off the image of his Dad and his T.V. and never looked back.

Do you believe you can change?

Have you increased the level of challenge, change and learning in your life? Or, if you have only just read the last three chapters, do you seriously intend to put this into action in your life?

Do you believe that you *can* make some changes in your way of life? Are you capable of meeting new challenges and engaging in new learning? Let's have a look at your self-belief in these areas.

Answer the following questions. Again, take 'work' to mean paid work, voluntary work, or work in the home.

Are you confident that you can make changes in your social life if you decide to?   Yes ☐ Maybe ☐ No ☐

Do you feel sure that you can develop new interests and leisure activities?   Yes ☐ Maybe ☐ No ☐

Would you be able to take on a work challenge now (such as learning a new skill or taking on a new role in an organisation)?   Yes ☐ Maybe ☐ No ☐

Could you sit down and learn about something that interested you if you chose to? Yes ☐ Maybe ☐ No ☐

Do you feel confident that you could study and pass a test or exam as you did when you were young (such as a driving test or school exam)? Yes ☐ Maybe ☐ No ☐

If someone sprung something on you – for instance an out-of-the-usual journey or an unusual social event – are you confident that you could rise to the challenge? Yes ☐ Maybe ☐ No ☐

Do you feel pretty positive about change in your life and feel able to deal with it? Yes ☐ Maybe ☐ No ☐

Do you believe that you are as open to learning now as you were when you were younger? Yes ☐ Maybe ☐ No ☐

Do you believe that you can learn pretty much as readily as you did when you were young (albeit that maybe you need to put in a bit more effort now)? Yes ☐ Maybe ☐ No ☐

Do you believe that you can change at your age? Yes ☐ Maybe ☐ No ☐

Calculate your score. Give yourself two for every 'Yes', one for every 'Maybe' and nought for every 'No'.

💡 **14-20:** You have the self-belief to make the changes that you think are worth making in most areas of your life. In the main, you are still open to the challenges that you faced as a younger person, and you are also open to change. You are not afraid of learning, and you haven't ruled yourself out because of preconceptions about what you should do at your age. This readiness for challenge, change and learning is a vital ingredient in doing the mental training necessary.

7-13: You aren't totally confident of your ability to meet challenges and deal with changes. You aren't sure about learning either. This may be because you have had some experience of this recently, and didn't fare as well as you thought you might. More likely, though, you are simply doing less of these things than you were when you were in your teens and twenties. Maybe you are out of practice, and it is this that is sapping your confidence. People who are out of work for a long period – for instance for parental leave or during a long illness – often suffer quite significant loss of confidence in their ability to do the job once they come back. This is quite normal and might simply be because you have had much less challenge, change and learning than you had when you were young. You might want to re-examine your self-belief in this respect.

0-6: You aren't at all confident that you can face up to challenges or changes, and you also doubt your ability to learn. This will be an obstacle to making brain-stimulating changes in your way of life. Why do you believe this? Are you buying into some outmoded notion of what people of your age can or cannot do? How do you know that you cannot do these things? Have you tried? Could it be that you are simply out of practice, and that your lack of confidence is caused by this? Whatever the reason, it is very important that you overcome this lack of self-belief when you try to make changes in your way of life, and try to learn new strategies of mental sharpness. Everyone at any age can learn, cope with change, and meet challenges. If you think that you cannot, this is not a reality – it is a false belief.

Do you want to change?

No matter whether you believe you can change now that you are over 50, an equally important question is whether you want to change.

Anyone over 50 faces challenges and changes whether they like them or not. There is a temptation to slip into thinking that we can ease off the accelerator a little at work and in other areas of our lives.

This way of thinking is a bit like a Trojan horse, however. Just as you can get 'Trojan' viruses in your computer – damaging mini programs that slip into your computer system on the back of other more benign software – so you can get Trojan mental viruses – age-related thought and behaviour patterns.

Change is not optional

If you don't embrace change, then change will embrace you. Nothing in life stays the same. While you can try to think, behave and eat yourself younger, you can't ignore the inexorable biology of ageing.

The older you become, the greater the chance you have of suffering some significant illness, of losing people close to you and of having more or less enforced changes in your work life. None of these changes can be avoided. But if you have trained yourself to meet challenges and to continuously learn, then you will be much better able to cope with externally-imposed changes as they come on you.

Your closest relationships are not static either. They change when a child grows up and leaves home or starts to have boyfriends/girlfriends. They change when one person gets a new job, or gives up paid work, or becomes ill, or when finances change dramatically.

Your closest relationships are your biggest potential ally in creating a way of life that will stimulate your brain and keep you mentally younger.

When you were 17, you were on a steep learning curve where human relationships were concerned – sometimes giving joy and pain in equal measure. You didn't take these relationships for granted, and you were always learning, meeting the challenges and changing as you discovered who you were through your interactions with other people.

You may have found a soul mate and settled into the happy constancy of a long and stable relationship. But even the strongest relationship can't maintain such a positive tone unless there is fairly regular re-assessment and adjustment to the changing realities of life in a partnership.

Relationships have to embrace challenge and change, and be open to learning in much the same way that our ageing brains have to if they are going to maintain their sharpness.

Learning – and learning how to learn

Three years ago I was asked to present part of a television series on the topic of 'Learning how to learn'. I had relatively little television experience – mostly interviews – and had virtually no experience of presenting directly to camera.

I found myself in a studio, facing a camera, with a five-minute script in my hand. There was no autocue, so I had to memorise chunks of the script and present them to camera. It was an excruciating experience. I was horrified how hard it was to commit even a few sentences word perfect to camera.

Take after take, I stumbled over my lines, until at last, after several sweat-filled hours, the first five minutes were completed. That was the first of 12!

I had just turned 50, and was downhearted at what I felt was real evidence of the loss of my youthful mental powers. It got a little easier as the recordings went on, and I was mightily glad – as were the entire studio crew, I imagine – when the series was finished.

A year later, the same production company asked me to do a second series. My heart sank – I really couldn't imagine going through that torture again. Vanity overcame these doubts, however, and I embarked on the second series.

I was taken aback to discover how relatively easy it was to learn my first script. I can't quite pinpoint what the difference was – perhaps less anxiety, maybe more confidence. Or it could be that my brain had just become used to a type of learning that it hadn't engaged in much for several years.

It showed me personally what I have found in scientific studies: the more you learn, the more you can learn. With my colleagues at Trinity College Dublin, I have recently carried out a study with a group of over fifties who had to learn by heart several thousand words of text (prose, poetry, songs, sport facts – anything they were interested in) over six weeks. We found significant changes in both their brains and their ability to learn new information[17].

So when you are trying to think yourself into a 10-years-younger frame of mind, don't be put off by feeling that you won't be able to learn, or that you don't have the ability to face up to change or challenge. Only once you have practised will you be able to judge what you are capable of. The very act of learning and adapting will enhance your ability to learn.

Staying motivated

It can be hard to keep up a physical exercise programme. Unless you feel good after exercise, it is difficult to keep it up. You need some personal benefit – sport, hobbies, attractiveness to others, family activities, for instance – to maintain physical fitness training. If you have a clear purpose in staying physically fit, however, it is easier to stay motivated.

And the same is true for mental exercise. It is hard to go to the effort of mental training without some more immediate purpose.

To keep up your motivation, you should see some need for using this increased mental fitness in your everyday life. When you were young, you were constantly challenged to perform – whether in education, the job market or generally finding your way in the world.

Though many of us can have these kind of challenges later

in life, they tend to occur less often. If you have been doing the same job for 20 or 30 years, it's often very easy to keep doing it with the minimum of mental challenge. If you are financially secure, there is no external reason to do that course or learn that skill. Retirement can mean the comfort zone of familiarity, routine and – above all – little challenge and few demands made on you.

To be motivated to build mental fitness, you have to tie your fitness programme to goals and challenges in your life that are satisfying and rewarding for you. Having reviewed your own self-image, commitment and motivation in this chapter, go back over the last three chapters on building challenge, change and learning in your life. Consider going through the exercises again, trying to keep in mind the possible mental viruses that are sapping your motivation and lowering your sights.

Sam managed to fight off his inherited mental virus: he woke up one morning with the awful vista of his father's face lit by the blue light of television on a winter's day and realised that the most complex object in the universe – the brain – could not be left to wither away from disuse. And the key feature of that object was something nothing else in the universe possessed – *free will*.

Sam never looked back and is currently thriving in the new prime of life.

Step 7:
Feed Your Brain –
Exercise and Diet

Tony and George

'Did you find somewhere to park?' 'Yes, but it was quite far away and the meter runs out at 11. Will we be finished by then?' He is a little breathless and flushed. He walks into the room and sits heavily in the chair, his spine curved against its straight back. He pulls his jacket open. 'Take it off if you like,' I say. He moves to stand up, then sits back with a sigh. 'No, I'm fine – you should get a lift in this place, those stairs are murder.' He is still sweating, and his breathing isn't quite back to normal. He is a bit overweight and his skin is pale. 'Didn't really want to come today,' he says. 'It's my birthday.' 'Ah, sorry about that, how old are you?' 'Fifty-five,' he says. 'Many happy returns, George,' I say.

He is removing the clips from the bottom of his trousers as I come out to meet him. I take his hand, noticing it is tanned, like *his face, and his grip is firm. He is short and wiry, and walks quickly into the room ahead of me, taking a seat, straight-backed on the chair. He has incredibly bright and alert eyes. 'Thanks for coming,' I say. He says, 'Don't worry, I'm just back from a ride.' 'A bike ride?' I ask. 'Yes, just 20 miles because I was coming here.' 'Twenty miles, before 10 in the morning – how far do you normally ride?' 'Ah, not much now – not like when I was younger – I wouldn't do more than 50 or 60 miles in a day now.' 'Fifty or 60 miles?' I gulp. 'How old are you?' 'Seventy five next week,' he says. 'Many happy returns, Tony,' I say.*

These two real people were 20 years apart in chronological age. Tony was the older but in their bodies the situation appeared reversed. If I had taken a video of the two men coming to my office, and then blanked off their faces, I am certain that you would have judged George to be the older and Tony the younger man.

I say that because of a number of factors. Weight wouldn't be the main one, because being overweight is as much a feature of youth these days as of age. Posture was one reason. Tony was erect, albeit with slightly rounded shoulders from crouching over the handlebars of his bike. Sitting in the chair in my office, his back was straight. George, on the other hand, had a hunched, slumped sort of posture.

Another factor was the speed with which they moved. Tony moved quickly – *sprightly* would be a good way to describe it. He carried himself rather as young athletes move – a sort of glide. George, on the other hand, seemed aware and slightly oppressed by gravity in a way that wasn't entirely due to his weight.

If you have ever met a top- or even intermediate-level athlete, you will no doubt have noticed an indefinable quality they have – they radiate a *sheen*. It may partly be the posture, which is superbly erect, but it is also the skin and eyes. They have a *sharpness* about them that seems reflected in the crispness of their speech and the briskness of their movements.

Tony had a bit of that ineffable sheen and sharpness. George did not. Physical fitness has obvious effects on the body that are visible to everyone. It would be astonishing if the brain were exempt from these positive effects. It is not. In fact, the brain is exquisitely sensitive to the beneficial effects of exercise, as is explained in the boxes in this chapter.

The impression I had that Tony was mentally sharper than George fits with the evidence of people who have been physically fit and active for long periods in their lives. On average, these over-fifties are indeed mentally sharper, more intelligent, have better memories, stronger reasoning ability and excellent powers of concentration[18].

People over 60 who are physically active and fit are less likely to show a decline in mental ability over time[19] and even a four-month exercise programme can boost mental faculties such as memory, concentration and attention.

Those who are physically fit also tend to pay more attention to what they eat, and this may be another factor contributing to this sheen. Take a close look at your level of exercise and at your diet. These not only have proven and very considerable effects on your brain and mental sharpness but also on your general health.

Do you take enough exercise?

Throughout this book I have been making the point that what older people *do* may be as important a factor in how much they age as their number of years on the planet. Younger people tend to do more physical activity, so perhaps ageing is exaggerated in those older people who get out of the habit of it. This certainly seemed to be true for George.

It's not just in formal, planned physical activity such as walking, jogging, sport or gym where younger people are more active. They also use public transport more, move around more, and do a wider range of general activities. All this is exercise.

In the table opposite, try to estimate how often you engage (or have engaged) in the types of physical activity listed. Use the scale shown for each activity. For example, if, when you were under 20, you played sport once or twice a week, put a three in the 'under 20' box opposite 'sport that raised your pulse'. If you hardly ever did any recreational walking when you were under 20, then put in nought opposite that. Do this for all the types of exercise listed, then add up the total level of activity when you were under 20. Now do the same for each of the other periods in your life.

How do your scores compare over the different periods of your life? Many people – but not all – show a great reduction in their level of physical activity as the years go on. While in part this may be for medical reasons, mostly it is just habit.

	Under 20	21–40	42–60	Over 60
Sport that raises your pulse significantly (such as tennis, soccer)				
Sport that doesn't raise your pulse significantly (such as golf, fishing)				
Gym				
Recreational brisk walking for its own sake – at least two miles				
Walking to get somewhere (such as the train station, shop, bus) for at least half a mile				
Running or jogging				
Swimming				
Vigorous gardening (such as heavy digging, manual hedge clipping)				
Vigorous household work (such as heavy DIY, housework)				
Sex				
Dancing				
TOTAL				

0 – never

1 – once or twice a year

2 – once or twice a month

3 – once or twice a week

4 – once or twice a day

Staying youthful means behaving more like a young person. If your physical activity scores show a decline over the decades, then you should consider trying to increase your physical activity levels.

Make an exercise plan

If you are happy with your current level of physical fitness, that is fine. You don't have to be like Tony, cycling 20 miles before breakfast, but you might like to check whether your level of fitness is optimal for your age. You might like to consider joining a gym or health club. A fitness instructor will assess your level of fitness and suggest a programme that is suited to your physical condition and age.

Don't be put off by the fact that the gym may be full of people under 50: this just illustrates my point that how old you are depends a lot on what you do. Going to the gym is one way to stay youthful. Why shouldn't you become more youthful by doing this?

In the chart opposite, put a tick next to those forms of exercise that you might consider starting or increasing, and note down what you might do specifically to improve your physical fitness.

Now plan the steps you need to take to start this new or increased level of activity and write them down in the chart opposite. Getting started is always the hardest bit. Write down any step that will take you nearer the activity. This might involve phoning a club or a friend, looking up a website or buying a new pair of running shoes. Getting a friend or partner involved can help build the motivation you need and make it fun.

	Tick here if you will consider this	Note here the first steps you'll take to start or increase this (eg phone call to club/centre; book lesson; buy equipment; discuss with friend)
Walking		
Jogging		
Swimming		
Home maintenance		
Tennis		
Badminton		
Aerobics		
Aqua-aerobics		
Golf		
Bowling		
Table-tennis		
Gym		
Weights		
Gardening		
Cycling		
Yoga		
Other		
Other		
Other		
Other		

Aerobic exercise

Aerobic exercise is any physical activity that makes you sweat and raises your heart and breathing rate to a sustainable level for a continuous period of 15 minutes or more. For example, walking at a fairly brisk pace, cycling or jogging are all aerobic – provided you can maintain the pace. If you become breathless or your muscles start to ache you are no longer exercising aerobically and should slow down.

Do you eat well enough?

Nutritionists tell us that diet is a big factor in our vulnerability to diseases like cancer and heart disease. What they don't tell us so clearly is that your brain is also affected by what you eat.

Fish, vegetables and fruit – particularly dark fruit such as cranberries and blackcurrants – are vital for a healthy brain. Eat lots of them – as part of a balanced diet and without

EXERCISE AND THE BRAIN

Aerobic exercise has hugely positive effects on the brain – especially in those aged over 50[20]. The longer you stay physically fit, the more marked the effects. But even after just four months, a modest aerobic training programme with a group of over sixties found improvements in a number of key mental abilities. A control group who went through a strength and flexibility programme only didn't show the same improvements.

A group of over sixties who took part in a regular aerobic training programme for three years showed none of the decline in mental abilities seen in a control group of over sixties during the same period[21].

It seems that aerobic exercise boosts a key region of your brain – the frontal lobes. This region is essential for mental sharpness because it is involved in our ability to organize ourselves, make decisions, show initiative, have a sense of humour, pay attention, and remember if we have already told that story before we tell it again!

The frontal lobes make us who we are. The problem is, this is the region of the brain that ageing attacks most. This is one reason why we tend to become forgetful, slow on the uptake and prone to repeating ourselves in old age. But the good news is that aerobic exercise can prevent a lot of this decline in mental faculties.

Exercise generates a chemical called BDNF (Brain-derived neurotrophic factor). BDNF acts like a fertiliser for new brain connections and new brain cells. Physical fitness also increases the amount of serotonin in the brain, which is not only a key brain chemical for enhancing positive mood, but also helps brain cells to proliferate. Exercise also causes new capillaries – tiny blood vessels – to sprout in the brain, increasing the nourishment – and hence survival – of brain cells and their connections that might otherwise wither under the pressure of ageing. Scientists have discovered that running boosts the growth of nerve cells too. One study found that the brains of mice that exercised had about two and a half times more new nerve cells than those of sedentary mice.

In other words, for the over-fifties, exercise is a sort of wonder-drug that makes you more mentally agile, less forgetful and delays the loss of sharpness that would otherwise occur.

going to excess, of course – and you will be doing your brain a favour and helping to keep your brain cells healthy and well-connected.

Foods high in saturated fats – such as potato crisps, most processed food and fried foods – dull your mental faculties and should be eaten in moderation only. Rats fed on the equivalent of burger and French fries show poorer memory and mental agility compared with rats that are fed on a less fatty diet[22]. Too much salt – again a feature of most processed foods – also blunts your mental sharpness and, like saturated fat, should be kept to a minimum.

Generally you should eat at least five portions of fruit and vegetables per day and, if you can, make one of these portions dark or red fruit (such as strawberries, raspberries, blackberries, cranberries and red currants). You should eat fish regularly as part of a balanced diet.

Think of the last three days: has your diet been good for your brain? Fill out the table.

	Yesterday	Day Before Yesterday	Previous Day
How many portions of fruit?			
How many portions of vegetables?			
Any fish?			
How many portions of fatty, processed food?			

If you eat healthily and become physically fit, you are likely to find your mental agility and alertness improve and you will become generally more mentally sharp.

DIET AND YOUR BRAIN

Fish oils — omega-3s in particular — help maintain brain cells and build stronger and better connections between them. Brightly coloured fruits and vegetables, such as strawberries, blueberries and spinach, can also help improve communication between brain cells and maintain healthy cells in the older brain.

These effects may arise in part from their high antioxidant content. Antioxidant molecules combat free radicals, highly reactive molecules produced by normal cellular processes that can harm brain cells and function. One four-year study involving a group of over sixties found that a diet high in the antioxidant vitamin E could lower the risk of Alzheimer's disease.

Foods that contain high levels of saturated fat, on the other hand, can impair brain function, including memory, and may slightly increase the risk of dementia. In part this may be because levels of the key 'brain fertiliser', BDNF (brain derived neurotrophic factor), are reduced by a diet high in saturated fats.

A third very important ingredient for keeping mentally sharp is to stay as relaxed and unstressed as possible. Let's turn to this next.

Step 8:
Learn to Relax and Reduce Stress

Christine and Mark

Christine leaned forward at her desk and rubbed her eyes. At the same time she felt the familiar knot of tension at the top of her spine, and also became aware that the muscles in her shoulders and neck were as tight as if she were carrying two heavy cases.

She glanced at the computer screen. Still 50 or so unanswered emails, and she still hadn't got the papers ready for tomorrow morning's meeting. Such a feeling of pressure – of never having enough time. She glanced at her watch – 8pm. Missed the supermarket – have to pick up a pizza on the way home – again.

Christine woke up at 5am, her heart racing and her mind spinning. Surely at age 55 and near the top of the tree at work, she could afford to relax and not spend her nights dream-worrying about her responsibilities? She dragged herself out of bed at 6am, took some paracetamol for her pounding headache and regretted the late-night bottle of red wine she seemed to need to unwind these days. She pulled on her clothes and hurried out to work to prepare for an 8am meeting.

Mark lay in bed, his eyes on the television but his mind somewhere else. The morning news had finished, he vaguely registered, and his finger flicked the remote through a succession of daytime soaps and shows.

The sky outside was grey: it had been blue the morning he retired. He was spending too much time in bed, but at least in bed he could avoid pacing about the flat trying to decide what to do next. He didn't seem to feel as anxious here as he did, fully dressed, in the sitting room with nowhere to go.

The pile of books on his bedside taunted him – whenever he started reading he found that after a couple of pages, while his eyes had been following the words, his mind had not. He managed the newspaper most days – just.

He had spent 40 years feeling that the world would stop if he didn't keep working hard. That was 40 years of thinking, eating, sleeping work. All out of proportion. Now he had a feeling of being lost, without bearings. And there was a terrible fluttering in his heart when the anxiety started.

Stress

Stress happens when the demands made on you are way out of kilter with your ability to cope with them. Or, more accurately, your *perception* of the demands and your ability. This is true for mind, brain and body. Too much mental or physical demand causes one kind of stress, too little causes another. Christine placed too many demands on herself, Mark too few.

Let's take Mark first. Before his retirement he had failed to develop the habits and skills needed to keep up the challenge, change and learning that could have made his retirement rich and enjoyable rather than dull and stressful.

Mark's anxiety – if prolonged over months and years – would have negative effects on his mind and body, as well as on his brain. The box, 'Stress and your brain' (page 123), explains how severe long-lasting stress can cause memory problems.

Fortunately, most of these effects can be reversed if the stress level is reduced, and the good thing about stress is that it is controllable.

Christine's stress may seem to be out of her control, because of all the demands made on her by her work. In fact, her stress is mainly due to the excessively high standards she sets for herself, and her over-estimation of how crucial she is to everything that goes on at work.

If you have a supercharged, all-competent, takes-responsibility-for-everything person in the workplace, that person's co-workers will – quite unconsciously – sit back and let them do most of the work.

This is what happened to Christine. As a result, her belief that she was indispensable and that everything would be chaos without her working herself into the ground seemed perfectly rational.

But Christine might be dismayed if she knew that during the three months she was away recovering from a broken leg, the office had managed to re-adjust to her absence quite well, and that her stress-producing workload was really not necessary.

So neither the demands nor the lack of demands made on you exist independently of your frame of mind and outlook.

The way you behave changes the world around you. What happens in the world in turn affects your perceptions and beliefs: these then influence how you feel, and in particular how stressed you feel. The chart below illustrates this cycle.

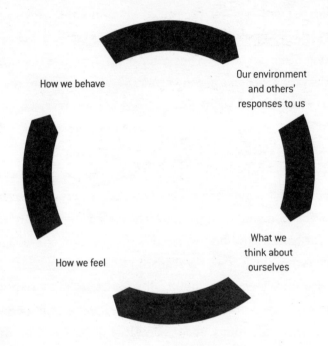

How we behave

Our environment
and others'
responses to us

What we
think about
ourselves

How we feel

Stress and challenge

If you set some challenges for yourself after reading some of the earlier chapters in the book, you might have felt a certain amount of stress. The very nature of challenge is that you are attempting something that is slightly beyond what you typically do at the moment.

Stress is the mismatch between what you think you can do and what's expected of you (including by yourself). Challenge means raising expectations a little, and so challenge can generate a little stress.

STRESS AND YOUR BRAIN

Moderate levels of stress can be energising and stimulating. But very high levels of prolonged stress – severe deprivation and poverty in an inner-city area for instance – can have serious negative effects on the brain. In particular, the memory organising centre of the brain – the hippocampus – is very sensitive to chemicals called glutamates that are pumped into the brain under stress.

When that stress is severe and prolonged, these glutamates can corrode some of the connections in the hippocampus and even cause the hippocampus to shrink. Veterans of the Vietnam war who had endured terrible battle conditions and had developed long-lasting post-traumatic stress disorder, for instance, tended to have a smaller hippocampus and poorer memory than other veterans. This may be one of a number of reasons why we suffer poor memory when we are stressed, though distraction and worry are likely to be much more significant. Fortunately, in most cases, these effects disappear when the stress lifts and memory and hippocampal size returns to normal.

But moderate amounts of stress can be enlivening rather than unpleasant, if you look at it in the right way. And these sensations of stress and mild anxiety caused by trying to do something challenging can rapidly turn to exhilaration if you master the challenge.

Mastering a challenge causes a surge of feel-good brain chemicals, enhances your self-esteem and makes it easier for you to meet new challenges and make changes in your life.

Below is a list of some of the symptoms of stress. Put a tick against those that you experience regularly.

- ·Ö· Butterflies in stomach
- ·Ö· Racing heart
- ·Ö· Sweating
- ·Ö· Tense muscles
- ·Ö· Dry mouth
- ·Ö· Sleep disturbance
- ·Ö· Difficulty concentrating
- ·Ö· Easily startled
- ·Ö· Irritable
- ·Ö· Restless

Many of these symptoms in a mild form can also be linked to feeling excited at the prospect of challenge or change. A person who interprets these feelings as fear may give up on the challenge and avoid the change. But if they make a slight mental shift and interpret them as excitement, then these 'symptoms' can become an ally rather than an obstacle.

Setting and achieving goals is a very important way of beating stress. The '*Yes!*' brain chemicals that spurt into your brain when you master a challenge are a wonderful antidote to stress. It's not the size or importance of the goal that matters: it's the fact that you set out to achieve something – anything – and did it. This can be as simple as enrolling in an evening class.

Mark's anxiety came partly from losing the goals that, throughout his life, only his job supplied. He had been over-focused on his work, and didn't give enough priority to other parts of his life.

Any of us would feel this kind of stress and anxiety if we woke up in the morning with nothing to aim for that day. Even if you don't enjoy work, the fact is that earning a pay cheque is the very real goal making you get out of bed in the morning.

Christine's problem is not too few goals and too little challenge – but the opposite. Such are the demands on her (imposed as much by herself as by her employer) that she doesn't make time and mental space for developing other parts of her life.

This is a very common problem in Western society, and you *must* begin to tackle it in your fifties if you are going to thrive over the next 30 years – a period, remember, which has the potential to be the prime of your life.

Assess your goals

Tick the statement below which fits your situation most closely.

1. I have a lot of different goals in different areas of my day-to-day life and always have something to aim for. ❏

2. I have too many goals in different areas of my life – I find it hard to keep up with them and am under some stress as a result. ❏

3. I have goals, but they tend to be focused on either work or family, and I can see me losing these goals when I retire or when my family leaves home. ❏

4. I don't really have goals. I live pretty much day to day, taking things as they come. ❏

If answer 1 applies to you, that's good. For most people, goals are essential. And given that change is inevitable and constant, you really need to have goals in more than one area of your life to avoid Mark's situation.

If you chose 2, then you need to do some time management and prioritisation. You can't do everything. Ask yourself this: if you were told you had only two years to live, which of these goals would you hold on to, and which would you abandon or downgrade? As one sage noted with regard to life – this is not a rehearsal.

Of course, it isn't possible to live one's life as if we only had two years to live. What students, for instance, would bother to study for their final exams under these circumstances? But if you are over-stressed by having too many goals, the exercise can be very useful in helping sort out your key goals from the less important ones.

If you chose 3, then you, like Christine, are in danger of suffering a real jolt when you leave work or work leaves you. You face a similar problem if your life is focused round your family rather than work, for, almost inevitably, your family will develop independent lives. The sooner you can start to diversify – with the help of the challenge, change and learning steps earlier in this book if you like – the better prepared you will be for these changes.

If 4 applied to you, you may be very happy and contented. If you are contented, however, it is likely that you have at least some goals that are so well-ingrained that you don't think of them as such. For most people, goals – even very modest ones – are pretty essential for keeping a mental balance in life.

Apart from the stress, as you saw earlier, goals are an

essential part of challenge, and mental challenge is key to staying sharp over 50. So if you really don't have any clear goals, go back over the challenge, change and learning steps earlier in this book. Work out at least one or two small goals and then pinpoint what steps you have to take to achieve them.

Stress and control

Earlier on I explained how stress arises from a mismatch between the demands put upon you and how you see your ability to cope with these demands. *'How you see'* is the key phrase here. Demands – like beauty – are in the eye of the beholder.

In one study, people were asked to work on a task that demanded a lot of concentration. This task was made even more difficult by the level of distracting noise they faced, and some of the volunteers said that they were feeling quite stressed by the demands made on them.

They were then told that they could switch off the noise if they wanted to by pressing a button. Their stress levels immediately dropped simply by knowing that they could push the button if they wanted to, even though they hardly ever did.

In other words, the stressfulness of demands made on you exists partly in reality and partly in your mind. If you have a sense of control – even *potential* control – over demands, this is a great antidote to becoming stressed.

There are limits of course to this. You may be in a job where the demands are, in reality, too great. Or you are perhaps looking after a disabled relative, and facing big demands but with relatively little control over these demands. However, you always have *some* control, no matter how demanding the situation. As a last resort, you can leave a job that is too demanding or make more time for yourself at home.

Even to think – *I don't have to put up with this, I can stop it if I want to* – can give you some sense of control, as was the case for the people in the noisy office.

If you are stressed at work you could:

🔆 Seek a meeting with your manager to discuss your workload.

🔆 Delegate some of your tasks and prioritise the most important.

🔆 Consider whether you are setting unreasonable demands on yourself in your eagerness to seek promotion.

🔆 Perhaps reconsider your lifestyle if workload/overtime is a consequence of maintaining heavy financial commitments – perhaps reduce your expectations (foreign holidays/new car) in favour of a less stressful life.

At home you could do the following to reduce stress:

🔆 If household demands are too great, try to get others to share in the tasks, or set your sights lower.

🔆 If caring for an elderly or disabled relative is putting you under stress, seek additional help/respite care (after all, who will be the carer if you make yourself ill?).

Unreasonable demands usually arise because of the unreasonable expectations of people who hold some sort of power over you. Less dramatic than thinking about leaving is telling the person in charge that their demands are unreasonable and that you want them to change.

The response to this can never be predicted with certainty, but you might find your sense of control strengthened by facing the challenge of speaking up. If you are surprised by the response, it may be that you are, in part, responsible for the demands made on you. Perfectionists, for instance, often behave as if the others are driving them to become stressed-out by overwork, when in fact the tyrant inside their own head is the real culprit.

Fear of rejection can be another potent reason why people don't speak up. 'They won't like me any more' would be a common thought in the mind of someone putting up with unreasonable demands.

A feeling that *this is not fair* can also in some cases cause unnecessary stress. The belief that nature should be fair can cause as much distress. The jargon for this is the *'just world hypothesis'* – a mistaken belief that there is some fundamental principle of fairness in the natural world against which one's circumstances should be judged – 'Why should I get this illness?', 'Why did this accident happen to *my* family?'

There is no such principle in the natural world, and there are no absolute standards against which one can judge one's lot in life. But if you believe that the natural world should be fair or just, then it is not difficult to drive oneself into a continuous state of frustration and demoralisation at the unjustness of one's fate.

Feeling that fate has dealt with you unjustly can perpetuate a sense of not being in control, and can increase stress. People who believe that the natural world should be fair, but that they have been treated unfairly by it, tend to adjust poorly to disability and other misfortunes. If you accept, on the other hand, that nature has no interest in being fair, then you can much better accept your situation and seek to gain what control you can over it.

This does not of course apply to the social world to the same extent: a person disabled in an accident may become a strong campaigner for disabled rights without believing herself to have been dealt an unfair hand by Mother Nature. You can influence the world that mankind has created but you cannot control nature or chance to the same extent.

Exert control

Think about the sources of stress in your life – we all have some. In the table below you'll see some different areas of your life, and some questions about how much control you have exerted over each source of stress. For any areas of your life where you experience stress, put a tick in the box that best describes how much control you feel over the situation.

	Source of stress					
	Relationships	Health	Family	Work	Money	Quality of life
I definitely cannot exert control over this						
I don't think I can exert much control over this						
I could perhaps exert some control over this						
I could almost certainly exert quite a lot of control over this						

Do you feel that you have any control over the stress in your life? If not, perhaps you should think again. Even if you have a very serious illness or disability, for instance, it is very likely that there is *something* you can do to reduce the stress it causes.

To take another example, even if you are very stressed by your work, it is likely that there are measures you can take (see page 128). Remember, stress exists partly in your perception and partly in the outside world. The example of Christine at the beginning of this step was a case in point.

It doesn't matter how tiny the step you take, or how small the reduction in stress it brings about, exerting some control – *any* control – can help break the vicious cycle of helplessness and inaction.

It is often hard to do this, because a big reduction in stress may seem unattainable and impossibly far off. In the chart below, write down the main source or sources of stress, if you have any, in your life.

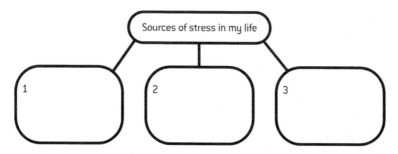

Sources of stress in my life

1

2

3

Now take each of these sources of stress in turn, and think of one very small way you can increase your control over that stress even a tiny extent. Christine, for instance, decided that she would not deal with emails from one particular department at work. Instead she would pass these on to someone else in her office, and simply delegate all except very important decisions to this one person. Though this made only a very small difference to her workload, it was an important start in feeling less swamped and out of control.

Mark made the decision that he would set his alarm and get up at a set time each weekday morning. He would dress smartly as if he were meeting someone, and he would go out and buy a newspaper and have a cup of coffee in the café. Though this did not dramatically or immediately change Mark's stress levels, it was a small but important first step towards taking control over his life in more significant ways.

Write in the chart below a source of your stress, along with one small step you could take to increase your control over it even slightly.

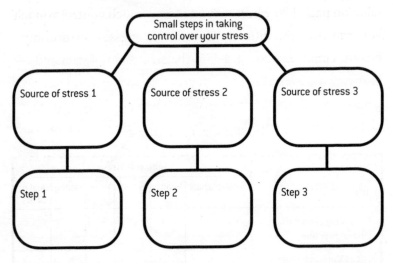

Once you have identified the small steps you can take, put them into action at the first opportunity. If necessary, repeat these steps several times. If you manage that, or if some of the steps don't work for you, try out some new small steps to gain control. Put these in the chart opposite.

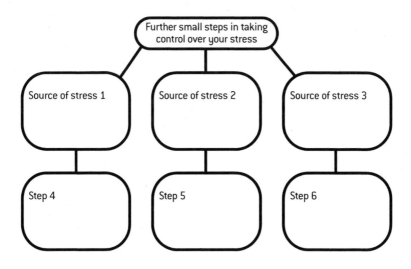

After you have tried this second set of steps, look back at the table on page 130 where you rated how much control you felt you had over the different domains of stress – relationships, health, family and so on. Fill in the table below again and see if any of your ratings have changed from the first time you completed the table. If not, don't give up. It is difficult to change habits, particularly habits of thinking, but you really

	Source of stress					
	Relationships	Health	Family	Work	Money	Quality of life
I definitely cannot exert control over this						
I don't think I can exert much control over this						
I could perhaps exert some control over this						
I could almost certainly exert quite a lot of control over this						

need to persevere with these or further steps to try to gain some control over the stresses you encounter.

Physical relaxation

Close your eyes and mentally check each part of your body for tension. Decide whether it is very tense, quite tense, quite relaxed or very relaxed. If you are not sure, check by trying to tense it up more than it is at the moment and then relaxing it – trying to increase the relaxation as it un-tenses.

Mentally go over your whole body. From time to time, open your eyes and put a tick in the box opposite the relevant part in the table below.

	very tense	quite tense	quite relaxed	very relaxed
Face				
Forehead				
Back of neck				
Shoulders				
Chest				
Back				
Stomach				
Groin				
Buttocks				
Legs				
Feet				
Arms				
Hands				

You might have to spend a few sessions getting the hang of this. Muscular tension is a major cause of headache and other bodily aches and pains. Most of the time we are simply not aware of where the tension is located in the body.

Learning to identify *where* you are tense is a big step towards learning to *relax* that tension. Holding muscles tense uses energy and is a major source of fatigue. Fatigue makes stress worse, and saps the energy needed to deal with the stress.

Every time you turn a page of this book, take a few seconds to check through these 13 parts of your body. Notice which parts are tense. Try to break the habit of tension by *increasing* the tension slightly and then *boosting* the sense of release as the tensed muscle relaxes.

There are many different ways of learning to relax physically. To break these habits of tension, you really need to practise relaxing the various groups of muscles in your body. Generally, it's best to set aside one or two 15–20 minute periods each day and to work at it until it is almost automatic. If you do that, it becomes a lot easier to do 'mini-relaxations' in everyday situations, from reading a book to walking down the street.

There are many commercially-available audio tapes, CDs and videos/DVDs that teach relaxation. Physical relaxation is also a key part of many disciplines such as yoga. You might like to try one or more of these to find the one that suits you.

Autonomic relaxation

Sweaty palms and rapid pulse are examples of stress-related activity in your autonomic nervous system. This system controls automatic processes in the body such as heart rate, breathing and temperature. One way of controlling this activity is by slowing your breathing. Take in a longish breath – not so deep that it is an effort – and then slowly let it out, relaxing the muscles in your body as you do so.

Do this a few times with your eyes closed, gently slowing your breathing a little and linking the out-breath to relaxing your muscles. Don't worry too much about your breathing – just try to relax into a slightly slower rate.

Physical exercise also helps to control autonomic activity. For example, particularly aerobic exercise: this raises your pulse in the short term, but afterwards the physiological effects help reduce some of the autonomic activity.

Too much caffeine from coffee and tea also can increase autonomic activity, so reducing your intake can help too.

Mental relaxation

Most of us have our own ways of switching off, such as music, exercise, reading, or talking to friends or family. These methods may not work so well when we are under stress, and worrying thoughts stream through the mind in a flow that's hard to stop. In this case, the technique of visualisation can help.

Imagining a pleasant scene – particularly when linked to muscular relaxation – can be a useful way of switching off from preoccupying thoughts. Think of a time when you were very relaxed and happy – and re-create this in great detail in your mind's eye.

You must set aside a quiet time and place and leave at least 15 minutes for a session. At first you'll find visualisation diffi-cult to do, and your mind will probably freewheel the first few times you try it. But if you persevere, slowing your breathing a little and relaxing your body, you should find that you can relax into the imagined details of the pleasant scene.

Like any of these methods, you must practise it several times before you'll know whether or not it will help you. There are many commercially available audio tapes and CDs offering this type of image-based relaxation training.

Another type of mental relaxation is called 'mindfulness training'. This is essentially a way of training yourself to attend to one thing – for instance, your breath as it goes in and out – in a non-forced way that will help still your mind.

The critical aspect of this type of training is that you don't use *effort* to keep your mind on your breath. Rather, you simply practise being *aware* of whether or not your mind is on your breath.

As it is normal for your mind to wander continually, rather than feeling annoyed with yourself if you find that your mind is not on your breath, you simply move your attention back to it. It doesn't matter if you have to do this every few seconds: what is important is being aware of your mind at all times and bringing your attention back to your breath in a relaxed way.

Many people find that if they practise this once or twice a day for 15 to 20 minutes, it helps them to feel mentally more relaxed and calm. Many yoga, meditation and related classes offer this kind of training in mental relaxation. Many religions also teach similar techniques. If stress or tension are problems for you, then search around, and you should find a method that suits you. Easing stress will help you on your route towards mental sharpness. Physical exercise is also a proven aid to stress reduction – it can boost your mental sharpness, both directly and by helping you to relax. If you skipped Step 7, you might like to go back and consider using exercise to help control your stress.

Step 9:
Improve Your Memory

'I'm so sorry, I've forgotten your name...'

The room was packed, people milling about with glasses of wine. Sally, the hostess, came over, leading another woman. 'Peter, this is Margaret – she used to live round the corner from you.' 'Hello Margaret,' he replied, and shook her hand. Peter and Margaret chatted for a while until Sally swept her friend off to meet someone else. Later, after another glass of wine, Peter found himself beside Margaret again – he felt more relaxed and ready to talk. He smiled brightly. 'Hello... ah...' He faltered. What was her name again? 'Margaret,' she said, smiling a little stiffly. 'So sorry, my memory's terrible...' 'I can't be terribly memorable,' said Margaret, huffily.

Simon sat staring at his notes. Surely at 59 he shouldn't have to study for exams like a 19 year old, he thought, grimly. It was 40 years since he had last had to sit an exam. But now he had no choice – he had to retrain to get a certificate. His job was at stake and he needed another couple of years at least to increase his pension fund to a reasonable level. But how could he remember all this stuff? His memory felt rusty and leaky at the same time. When he was young he had no problem studying, but now it was proving very tough. He wasn't sure he would be able to pass the exam, but he had to.

The doorbell rang. It was the first of Marion's book group arriving, this month's book under her arm. 'I thought it was great,' June said. 'What did you think of it?' 'Quite good,' Marion replied, 'but I read it a couple of months ago and haven't managed to read it again – I hope I can remember it.' Later on, the group were talking about the key scene in the swimming pool. 'What do you think was going on between them there, Marion?' June asked. 'You know, I can't even remember the swimming pool scene,' she said, lamely. 'Really – but that was the most memorable part of the whole book!' Carol said haughtily.

'Joe, could you go to the supermarket and pick up a few things for me?' 'Okay, what do you need?' 'I need some bread, milk, butter, cooking apples, black pepper... and some washing powder. Oh, and get the newspaper.' 'Fine, I'll be right back.' It only took him 20 minutes. 'Here we are.' He put the bag on the table. 'Oh Joe – where are the cooking apples? I needed them right now! Your memory's terrible!'

Peter, Simon, Marion and Joe are all over 50, and their memories are under strain in four different everyday situations. If you asked each of them about their memory, they would probably say that it wasn't as good as when they were younger.

HOW RESEARCHERS MADE PEOPLE MENTALLY YOUNGER

Almost 3,000 men and women aged between 65 and 94 volunteered for a training programme to increase their mental sharpness. A quarter of them were trained in the kind of memory strategies you'll learn about in this chapter, while another quarter were trained in problem-solving and reasoning. The third group were trained to speed up their reactions and mental decision-making using computerised game-like exercises that steadily increased in difficulty as they mastered each level. The final group were for comparison and were not trained at all. The training involved small groups and took place in 10 roughly one-hour classes over a five or six week period. Then, 11 months later, the volunteers were assessed again.

All else being equal, if you measure mental function in a group of people aged over 65, you'll find that – *on average* – the mental sharpness declines at a fairly steady rate. Over a decade, you would see a substantial drop in the average mental abilities of a typical group of over 65 year olds. This study was remarkable because with just 10 sessions of training, the trained group showed an *increase* in cognitive ability equivalent to the degree of loss of mental capacity that you would typically see over a 7–14 year period. The training, in other words, *on average* took about a decade off the cognitive age of these volunteers. Four booster sessions given a year after the end of training further enhanced problem solving and mental speed, leading to improvements that lasted another year at least.

You must remember that these volunteers weren't selected for their education or their lifestyles: many of them may not have practised the training much, if at all – and it is therefore likely that these average results concealed even more significant effects for highly motivated and educated people.

Most of us who are over 50 notice that our memories aren't as good as they were 20 or 30 years earlier. There are at least two reasons for this. First there are the changes in our brains that take place as we grow older – these parallel the changes in the body.

The second reason is that most of us use our memories much less than we did when we were 20. As you saw in the

' YOU KNOW... MY MEMORY JUST ISN'T WHAT IT USED TO BE...'

It's very interesting to compare the brains of older and younger people as they try to memorise things. Take a list of words like bread, couch, carrot, milk, fish, apple, chair, shelf, table. Take a few seconds to try to memorise these words. Give this to a group of 20 year olds to memorise, and their brains will show a healthy surge of activity in the left frontal lobe, as well as in the main memory centres of the brain deep in the middle, in a region called the hippocampus.

What happens in the brains of the 70 year olds? Well, for a start they won't be able to memorise long lists of words nearly as well as the 20 year olds. But why? A peek into their brains while they are memorising gives us a clue. The 70 year olds don't switch on the left frontal lobe nearly as much as the younger volunteers, and this is a likely reason why they don't remember as well[23].

Let's take another look at the list of words that you tried to memorise. Did you sort them out into categories to help you remember them? In other words, did you sort them in your mind into 'furniture' (couch, chair, shelf, table) and 'food' (bread, carrot, milk, fish, apple)? If you did, you would have found it much easier to remember them.

Older people, it seems, tend not to do this kind of mental sorting when they are trying to remember things – they don't actively sift, sort and categorise in the way younger people are prone to do.

So what happens when you give the older volunteers a hint and tell them to sort the words into categories when they are memorising them? Sure enough, their memories improve. Not only that, however, they also show reasonably youthful activity in the left frontal lobe of their brains as they memorise[24].

One of the reasons our memories let us down as we get older, then, is that we don't attack the information with the same brain vigour that we did when we were young. To speculate, it might be that we have got out of the habit of learning new things, and the brain circuits – in the left frontal lobe for instance – have become relatively inactive through disuse.

So what can we do to keep our memories in good shape as we get older? Well, the obvious way is to learn to process the things you have to remember by sifting, sorting and linking them to other things you already know. This is called 'depth of encoding', a principle discovered by the eminent cognitive psychologist Fergus Craik, of the University of Toronto.

He and his colleagues have conclusively shown that the more you mentally process the information you have to remember, the better you remember it. In part, this is very likely because mental processing of this type activates the frontal lobes, which in turn strengthen connections between different items stored in the memory banks in your temporal lobes.

earlier chapters, most of us have much lower levels of challenge, change and learning in our lives: coping with these depends heavily on our memories.

The good news is that you can use the second reason to help offset some of the effects of the first. We now know that it is possible to train your memory to take as much as 14 years off your cognitive age[25]. The box on page 141, 'How researchers made people mentally younger' explains how.

A word of caution

Not all of the factors that affect memory changes can be reduced by memory training. If you are unlucky enough to have a disease or injury affecting your brain, then training may be ineffective. If your memory problems are severe enough to be clearly noticeable to friends and family, you should seek medical advice before trying to improve your memory.

Use more of your brain when you learn

Your memory is very gregarious: it thrives on linking up different aspects of the information you are trying to remember. These different aspects will switch on various parts of your brain and, broadly speaking, the more areas of your brain you switch on as you try to remember something, the more easily you'll remember it later on.

First, I'll describe a particularly powerful way of improving your memory – using the mind's eye. I start with this because your ability to remember images is affected less by the ageing process, it seems, than are other types of memory.

This method may not suit everyone, so I will describe several other memory-enhancing methods after this. But even if you find some of them hard at first, it is worth persevering for a while. These are skills and, as you will remember from when you learned to swim or ride a bike, you can't learn a skill in one or two attempts.

Also, to really improve your memory, it's important that you master at least some of the methods I'm going to outline now. Try all of them, and then practise as many as you can, giving priority to those you are most comfortable with.

Before we start, answer these questions about your typical thinking style.

Are you a visualiser or a verbaliser?

Try this task devised by the eminent psychologist Alan Baddeley: close your eyes and, in your mind's eye, count the windows in your house.

To do so, you have to take a mental tour round your house. You create a mental image of each room, and see and feel yourself walking through the hallway or up stairs. This part of the task uses the *visualising* parts of your brain.

But you also had to keep count, adding up the number of windows as you took your mental walk. This part of the task uses the *verbalising* parts of your brain – in your mind's voice, you spoke out the numbers one, two, three and so on.

We need both types of thinking most of the time. 'Where did I leave my glasses?' To solve that problem, you have to visualise where you were last – a mental picture of you sitting on the couch watching television, for instance – as well as talking yourself through your movements prior to this: 'Now where was I before dinner?'

But different people tend to rely on these two types of thinking to different degrees, and you probably have a preference for one or the other. Answer these questions:

Do you often use the mind's eye to solve problems with mental pictures?
Yes ☐ No ☐

Can you easily see objects moving in your mind's eye?
Yes ☐ No ☐

Can you do arithmetic by imagining the numbers chalked on a blackboard?
Yes ☐ No ☐

Do you find it hard to make a mental picture of anything?
Yes ☐ No ☐

Do you prefer problems involving words (such as crosswords) to those where you have to use mental images (for example, will that wardrobe fit into the bedroom?)?
Yes ☐ No ☐

Is most of your thinking verbal, as if you were talking to yourself?
Yes ☐ No ☐

If you answered 'Yes' to the first three, and 'No' to the last three, then you are probably more of a visualiser than a verbaliser. If, on the other hand, you answered 'No' to the first three and 'Yes' to the last three, then you are probably more of a verbaliser. Many people will be a bit of both.

It's interesting to ask your family, friends and colleagues how they place themselves in that dimension. For instance,

I recently asked a colleague of mine, an eminent physicist, whether he thought mainly in words or in pictures, and he said, without hesitation, 'Pictures mainly.' An equally eminent philosopher colleague was similarly unhesitating when he responded, 'Almost entirely in words.'

If you are a visualiser you are probably going to find it easier to use your mind's eye to boost your memory. If you are a verbaliser, it is possible that you might get most benefit from learning to use mental pictures to improve your memory. This is the first part of the memory step below.

If you are a visualiser, you will be better at remembering pictures, and words that easily spark off images – such as 'rose' or 'tree' – than verbalisers. Whether you are a verbaliser or a visualiser, if you take the trouble to use your mind's eye to picture what you are learning, this will boost your memory for what you learned.

A word of caution, however: sometimes it can take time to create mental images, particularly if you are more of a verbaliser, and this can slow down learning. So you have to be choosy about where and when to use this strategy, at least until you are expert at it. This means that whether you are a verbaliser, a visualiser or a bit of both, it's important that you learn to use more than one memory strategy.

Some of the later memory tricks that I'll describe concentrate on the verbalising parts of the brain. So you can see from this that it is not the case that imagery is 'good' and verbalising 'bad'. They are both incredibly powerful tools and we need both to use our brains to their full extent.

At school, however, we learnt to rely on words much more than mental pictures, and most adults have lost much of the ability to think in pictures that they had as young children. Over 50, it is important to try to recapture some of that ability, because it can be a major help in making the most of your memory.

Here are two short descriptions. Read each of them to yourself, silently, and time how long you take.

1. *The cows' udders swung like heavy bells as they plodded, slip-slopping through the steaming newly-fallen dung of the leader. Their breath rose in the still, frosty air, smearing the crisp outline of the rising sun. The last cow reared and kicked as a large brown rat darted between its legs.*

2. *The sheep were more common in the relatively barren uplands, though the economics of sheep farming were becoming marginal, and these pastures were gradually returning to their native state. Though the visitors from the nearby city liked this, it was a tragedy for the farmers who had lost their livelihoods.*

Both these passages are 50 words. How long did it take you to read each one? It took me around 11 seconds to read the first, and eight seconds to read the second. This was in spite of the fact that the second one contained longer words.

As an adult, if you are a visualiser, then you are more likely to take longer on the cow passage than on the sheep one. If you are a verbaliser, the difference would be much less, and maybe even reversed. In general, visualisers take up to 25 per cent longer to read prose like the first passage than verbalisers, while on more abstract passages like the second one, they read at about the same speed[26].

But this isn't a disadvantage for the visualisers, because adult visualisers remember the high-imagery material better than the verbalisers, but are no worse on abstract text. This is probably because when the visualisers read, the information is stored more widely in the brain, in both the language circuits and in the mind's eye.

This is what you will do if you practise some or all of the methods in this memory step – you will store information over more areas of your brain, and as a result be able to remember it more easily when you have to.

Make mental pictures of what you want to learn

Read the following list of words twice. When you have read them, close the book and see how many you can remember – write them down on a scrap of paper. Now open the book and compare your list with the original

dog

chair

hat

cloud

car

umbrella

pen

hen

book

fish

Now read the next list. This time, try to picture the object in your mind as you read each word. Read the list just once, but make sure you have created an image of each object in your mind's eye. As with the first list, see how many you can remember – write the words down on a scrap of paper and then compare them with the original list below.

table

glove

pencil

plane

cat

eagle

briefcase

moon

flower

shirt

You may well have found that it was easier to remember the second list, though there can be exceptions. Some people find it hard to create visual images and so don't benefit from this technique. In general, however, we are more likely to remember 'dog' if we see it as an image, than if we see or hear it as a word[27].

One explanation for this is that seeing the picture gives you two brain activations for the price of one. Not only does the brain's language system store the concept 'dog', but the brain's visual image system (and maybe also its touch system) also stores a copy of an image of 'dog' via the mind's eye.

In other words, when you learn words that can also trigger visual or other images, you get twice the number of brain areas called into action. This may explain why you remember the picture of the dog better than the word 'dog'.

If you think you can use this method (remember, if you

are not a natural visualiser, it will be hard at first, but with practice you can improve the skill), try it in your everyday life. Here are some examples of how the four people at the beginning of this chapter used it:

Peter, concerned that he had offended someone he would have liked to get to know better, decided that he had to boost his memory for names by making a mental picture of the written name in his mind's eye when he met people. Each time he glimpsed a person, he would flash up that written name in his mind's eye.

Simon started to use visual images in studying for exams and, more generally, when reading manuals and documents necessary for his work. As a safety manager, he had to master new regulations and technical data. Instead of simply reading the material and trying to memorise it, he made the effort to make mental pictures whenever possible while studying. For instance, instead of just trying to remember the wording of the new regulations for dealing with electrical fires, he would create a mental image of the sparking electricity, the flames and the new type of extinguisher needed to douse them.

Marion improved her memory for the books she read by pausing every so often and making a vivid mental image of key scenes in the book. She would try to picture not only static views like that of the swimming pool, but would also try to visualise the actions of people, the expressions on their faces and the sounds of their voices. Of course, this slowed down her reading a bit, but she remembered a lot more about the stories and was able to contribute more to the book group.

Joe was able to remember everything he needed to buy at the supermarket after learning to use visual imagery. If he had to pick up fewer than seven or eight items, he would take a few seconds to picture them together. For instance, he visualised black peppers and cooking apples floating in milk, with a block of butter impaled on one side of the container, a loaf of bread on the other and a packet of soap powder held open above them, sprinkling down. The unusual nature of this image made it more memorable.

If you think you'd like to learn to use this method to improve your day-to-day memory, bear in mind that it isn't enough just to read through this section and then try it a couple of times while holding the book in your hands. That would be like going to the gym and expecting to get fit after half an hour on the treadmill. Here's what to do:

Choose an activity

First, pick an activity that you are going to use as your training ground to practise this method. Tick one or two items from the following list:

- ❏ Reading newspapers
- ❏ Reading books
- ❏ Reading work materials
- ❏ Shopping
- ❏ Meeting people/conversation
- ❏ Formal meetings
- ❏ Telephone conversations
- ❏ Study
- ❏ Listening to the radio
- ❏ Other

You should practise your visual imagery method at least 20–30 times before you decide whether or not it is helping you to remember. You could, for instance, try it two or three times a day over the next 10 days or so.

Test your visualisation skills

Before you start practising this visualisation, see how well you can make a visual image. Close your eyes and create a mental picture of your sitting room. Visualise the layout, the shapes and the colours. If you can't do this very well at first, take a rest and then try it a few more times. If necessary, have a look round your living room in between sessions and then close your eyes and try again.

Skim and prepare the images

Having sharpened your visualisation skills, the next technique is to link visual images with abstract information, such as written text or names.

If you chose reading newspapers as your training activity, for instance, pick an article and skim through it, looking for images that might go with the text. These might be the face of a politician, a courtroom, a particular city skyline or a pictured location on a map.

If you are preparing for a meeting at work or at the club, or in a voluntary capacity, prepare by skimming through the minutes of the last meeting, and make images linked to the items as I described for reading a newspaper.

If you have just come to a party, take a minute or two on

your own to visualise the faces of the people you have met, and create a mental image of them and their names. For each person, pick a few mental images linked to something you know about them or that they told you about. For instance, if someone mentioned that they had just been on holiday in France, picture that person against a Parisian skyline or a French cheese.

Make a summary slide show

Having got the gist of the newspaper article by skimming through it, put the story together in pictures in your mind's eye – a sort of mental slide show or cartoon strip. Run through the slide show in your mind's eye.

You can use the same technique for reading minutes or even filling out a complex form – say for insurance, banking or legal purposes. Skim through the minutes or form as you would skim through a newspaper article, and make mental images of key points (for example, visualise the key people or places referred to). Making mental images of dry bureaucratic information is clearly more difficult than doing the same thing of a massacre in Iraq or a celebrity wedding in LA, but it is still possible – with practice.

Combine the slide show with the activity

Now read the newspaper article again more thoroughly, but this time visualising the scenes and faces as they appear in the article.

Similarly, in the course of the meeting of the work, club or voluntary committee, combine the images you have made of the issues in the minutes, and call them to mind as you listen to the relevant people speak. You can also use this technique on the telephone, when obtaining instructions or information. Try to make a mental picture of at least some elements of what is being said.

At the party, when you bump into one of the people you met earlier on, call up the images you made of your earlier conversation with them, and knit them into the conversation you have now.

Now let's turn to an ancient and more specific use of mental imagery as a memory boost.

Method of loci

Your memory will improve to the extent that you link what you are trying to remember to a range of different thoughts, images and sensations. Imagery in the mind's eye is one of the most ancient and effective ways of doing this.

Many of these methods were developed by the ancient Greeks – they named them *mnemonics* – and they used them to impress friends and Senators by giving long and convincing speeches without reference to any notes. Given how important rhetoric was in classical Greece, this was a pretty powerful strategy for social advancement.

One method that the Greeks really liked was called the 'method of loci'. Try this ancient memory method yourself now.

Try to remember the list of words given below, but do it in the following way. Pick a path or route that you know well – from your house to the nearest shop, for instance, or from a car park or station to your place of work.

Do a mental walk along that route, to make sure that you have the image relatively clear in your mind.

Now, take each object listed below, and mentally lay it at a different location along the route, such as a corner, gateway or shop front.

Here are the words:

> *Spoon*
>
> *Glove*
>
> *Frog*
>
> *Cactus*
>
> *Spanner*
>
> *Mirror*
>
> *Cup*
>
> *Knife*
>
> *Hat*
>
> *Ring*

You can keep looking back at the list of words while you are placing the objects – you don't have to memorise them verbally first.

Did you manage to lay these out on your mental street? With your mind's eye, walk along this path again, and try to 'see' the objects in their places. Check your memory again against the list above.

This is a – literally – classic example of the power of the mind's eye in boosting memory. By visualising the words along a familiar route, you bind the memory traces for these words into a much bigger brotherhood of brain cells than if you just learn them in the normal way.

Peter learnt to use this method so he wouldn't forget people's names at parties. At the next party he was invited to, he would place each person he met at one of the points on the walk between his house and the nearest shop. Margaret was there again: he placed her on a plinth at the park gate opposite his house. He left the next person he met standing at the corner of the junction with the main road, and the next one outside the bank, and so on.

Simon walked the mental walk between his office and the train station, placing key facts from his text book – each a mixture of words and pictures where possible – at each point on the route. When that route got crowded with facts, he chose another route – between his home and the local shop – to leave others.

For the next book in her book group, Marion placed key scenes and characters in the book at various points on the route she walked between her office and the place she had lunch.

Before he went to the supermarket, Joe would place the items he had to buy at different points along the way there. When he got to the supermarket, he would retrace the route in his mind's eye, picking up the items one by one.

Another very old method of improving your memory is called the 'pegword method'.

Pegword method

To use this, you have to learn a nonsense rhyme off by heart. In this rhyme, each of 10 digits is linked with a rhyming object. Take a couple of minutes to memorise this:

One is a bun,
Two is a shoe,
Three is a tree,
Four is a door,
Five is a hive,
Six is sticks,
Seven is heaven,
Eight is a gate,
Nine is wine,
Ten is a hen.

The rhymes make this easy to learn. Make sure you have it off by heart before you read on.

You can now use the images linked to each number to remember lists of people, objects or other numbers. Imagine you're at a meeting and you have been introduced to 10 people. How on earth do you remember all their names? It's not too difficult, if you follow these seven steps.

1. Picture the people round the table or room in your mind's eye.
2. Try to generate an image for each of the people in the meeting, linked to the number pegwords. I've given a few examples below, but these are completely arbitrary – you can use any images you like.
3. Go round them in order, starting on your left. Suppose the first person is John. Imagine John biting into a huge bun, crumbs dribbling down his suit. If you like, you can add a link to your mind's ear – his mother's voice scolding him with, 'Oh, John, don't make such a mess.'

4. Say, the next on the left is Sheila, and use the 'two-shoe' peg to picture Sheila – for example sitting in a giant shoe. Again, you might imagine a voice asking, 'Where's Sheila?'

5. Joe is third on the left, and three-tree can easily generate an image of Joe sitting in the branches of a tree, with someone shouting up at him, 'Joe, come down!'

6. Peter is next, and 'four-door' could see him, for instance, swinging on the door like a child, chanting, 'Peter's swinging, Peter's swinging.'

7. Celia, in fifth place, could be having trouble with the bees from a hive buzzing round her. Fred in sixth place might be chopping sticks beside a roaring fire. Susan in seventh place might be sitting on a cloud, playing a harp. Colin in eighth place might be hammering at a gate, while Jean in ninth place could be slumped beside an empty wine bottle. Chris in tenth place might be sitting demurely with a hen roosting on his head.

You get the idea, no doubt. Though there is no need for bizarre or silly images, anything that you find funny or interesting will be better remembered because the faint ripple of emotion generated in your brain will recruit a few thousand more brain cells into the brotherhood of that particular memory.

Now try your own images, this time remembering the people round a table at dinner. They are all strangers, and you are struggling to remember their names, which are: Jill, Mark, Mary, Lorna, William, James, Felicity, Fiona, Mike, Steve.

The pegword mnemonic is also very useful for learning telephone numbers, passwords or PIN numbers for bank or credit cards.

You use them in exactly the same way as you would when learning lists of names or objects. Take the number 1982345. You can learn that by creating the image of all the objects related to these numbers in a row. Namely: bun, wine, gate, shoe, tree, door, hive.

At first this will take longer than learning the numbers in your usual way. But with practice, you'll get much better at using your mind's eye in this way, and not only will you remember numbers more quickly, but you'll be much less likely to forget them.

Simon used the pegword method to learn key facts in his textbook, especially when they were in a particular order. He would make a visual image linking the fact with the number and its image – one-bun, two-shoe and so on.

Use your other senses to improve your memory

Using visual images of words is just one way to bind memories into your brain cells. Smell, sound, touch and taste can be just as effective. You can also imagine bodily movements or sensations. Try yourself with these words that are linked to various senses.

Cheese	Coffee	Smoke	(smell)
Ice	Sponge	Wool	(touch)
Laughter	Choir	Snore	(sound)
Spade	Racquet	Axe	(bodily movement)
Mint	Vinegar	Chocolate	(taste)
Hunger	Cold	Pain	(bodily sensations)

Generally, most people find vision the easiest sense to use as memory glue, with sound a close second. But everyone is different, and you might have the ability to use touch, movement or some other sensory modalities to link to information that you want to remember.

Make a soundtrack for your slide show

One way to use sound would be to make a soundtrack for your slide show by adding sounds to the pegwords:

One is a bun – imagine the sound of someone chewing.

Two is a shoe – hear in your mind's ear the sound of footsteps on a hard floor.

Three is a tree – create a sound image of a tree rustling and creaking in a high wind.

Four is a door – hear the door slam.

Five is a hive – imagine the heavy drone of bees on a hot summer day.

Six is sticks – hear someone cracking sticks to make kindling for a fire.

Seven is heaven – imagine celestial music.

Eight is a gate – a creaky gate swings open, rattling.

Nine is wine – a rich red wine gurgles out of the bottle and splashes gently into the glass.

Ten is a hen – hen clucking.

If you are trying to memorise something – say the names of a row of people around a table – you will remember their names better if you use the pegword method to create a visual image of each one linked to the face and name and *also* create a sound in your mind's ear to go with that image. This is because in storing up that memory, you are making brain cells fire in both the visual and auditory parts of the brain. The more brain cells that are active at the time you stored the memory, the more firmly will it be glued into your mind.

Use mental multimedia

Other senses can help as well. Suppose you meet someone called John Furlong. You can remember his name by visualising a long fur wrapped around his face. But you can also take a second to imagine the feel of that long fur around your own neck.

That simple and apparently silly exercise will make it more likely that you remember his name in future because now you are also causing cells in the touch centres of the brain to spring into action.

To stick with the example of people's names, suppose you met someone called Mary Coldsten. Not only could you visualise her as shivering in the cold and hear her teeth chattering – you could also imagine yourself feeling cold in her presence. If you took a couple of seconds to create this multimedia image, you can be pretty confident that you'll remember her name the next time you meet her.

Here are some examples of how the four people at the beginning of the chapter used soundtracks and multimedia to help make their memories more efficient.

Multimedia with soundtracks for people's names

When Peter met someone, he practised visualising their face and name and also replaying in his mind's ear the tone and quality of their voice. In Margaret's case, for example, he would pay attention to the low, husky nature of her voice as she said her name.

This isn't something we normally do: as you'll see later, we have only a limited attention span, and we mostly learn only what we need to.

When someone tells us their name, we normally register the word only, and sometimes we don't even pay much attention to that – hence we forget it 10 seconds after we've been told.

Paying attention to the sound of someone's voice saying a particular word or phrase is more something that a professional actor or mimic would do. Taking that extra couple of seconds to attend to the sound adds a soundtrack to your memory and hence makes it stick in your mind.

Peter practised the visual image technique on its own at first, and once it was more or less second nature, he began to practise adding a soundtrack to the slide show of people he met. Peter seldom forgot key names after that.

Multimedia with soundtracks for studying and reading

After he had become used to using visual images to help him remember the material he had to learn for his exams, Simon started to put soundtracks to the study slide shows that he made.

This isn't always easy – particularly for highly abstract facts such as rules and regulations. Imagine, for instance, trying to create a multimedia mental slide show of the licensing regulations for the use of Microsoft software.

Yet it can be done. For a start, Simon began to try to create a soundtrack of the voice of his lecturer in the class he attended on Tuesday and Thursday evenings. He would add this sound to embellished images of the slides that the lecturer presented, as well as to the shorthand images that he created himself while studying.

For instance, he was learning how to make the systems in his office audit-ready. The instructions were dense and dry, full of words such as 'quantifiable', 'procedures', 'protocols', 'service levels' and so on.

It's not easy to make visual or sound images of such abstract words, but you can add your own bizarre links to key ones. For instance, you might imagine the grey-suited consultant who is lecturing you singing one of these bloodless sentences like a swaggering Italian tenor …*Pre .. para..tion for an aud –it compris-es three key sta…..ges….*'

Simon liked opera and wasn't madly keen on audit procedures, so this was his quirky way of enlivening the material he had to learn. When he added an image of the consultant in tights and plumed hat to this slide show, he had no problem remembering the procedures for the audit.

Marion added soundtracks to the mental slide shows she made of the books she was reading. She had never done this before, but as well as creating visual images of how the characters looked, she also made sound pictures of their voices.

She would also try to hear in her mind's ear the sounds

linked to the passages she was reading. She was more likely to have remembered the swimming pool scene, for instance, if she had taken time to add a soundtrack of splashes to the crucial dialogue of the characters.

Joe made sure he remembered the shopping items – and indeed managed to increase the number he could remember without a note – by making a soundtrack to go with the visual images of some of the items – crunching of an apple, grinding of pepper, gurgling of milk and rhythmic humming of the washing machine, for instance.

Using your body to remember

Our world is dominated by sight and sound, probably because of film, television and music. This will change as engineers and scientists learn to stimulate our other senses – touch, taste, smell, bodily sensations and bodily movement. It's already here with virtual reality.

This will happen more and more over the next few years, and our over-reliance on vision and sound will lessen. In many non-Western cultures, smell and touch are as important as sight and hearing. In Western societies, these incredibly powerful capacities in our brain are greatly diminished through lack of training and use.

But very large areas of your brain are devoted to these senses, and you can still use them to boost your memory. It is well worth trying to develop the ability to use other senses as an aid to memory and not just rely on word, sight and sound.

Touch and movement

We remember the things we do much better than things we read, are told, or see. Think back to physical things you have done: a fairground ride, speaking your first words of Spanish in Barcelona, sailing a boat for the first time, taking a bungee jump, skiing, putting brush to paper and so on.

But much of our life we are sitting at desks, in armchairs and in cars. And most of the time our physical activities are routine and so well-practised that we hardly pay attention to what we are doing. These actions don't help us remember much, as we don't attend to routine things. But, as you know, we have to attend if we are to learn.

If I tell you how to do something, you will probably pay attention to the words I am speaking, but it is unlikely that you will really attend to the full meaning of the words.

For instance, suppose I tell you that to link your new printer to your computer, you must do this: go to the start menu, click on 'control panel', then on 'printers'; click on 'add new printer' and so on.

What do you do when confronted with instructions like this? Do you read them carefully, then close the book and just do it? Certainly not, at least not if you have never done this before.

Rather, you pull up your sleeves and work through the steps with the manual in hand. In other words, you learn by doing, not just by reading or watching.

If you only read the instructions, are interrupted, and then try to do the job the next day, you probably won't remember a thing. If you have acted out the steps, however, you are more likely to remember how to do it.

So much of our lives revolves round words rather than actions, however, that you might think that using your body has a limited role in memory. Perhaps not. Let's go back to the pegword method.

Use body pegwords

Read the list of pegwords below and try to come up with a body-related sensation to go with each one of them. Use anything other than sight or sound. For example, use touch, taste, smell, bodily sensation or bodily movement.

Try to think of an image in some or all of the categories, and jot this down in the table opposite each word.

	Touch	Taste	Smell	Bodily sensation	Bodily movement
One is a bun					
Two is a shoe					
Three is a tree					
Four is a door					
Five is a hive					
Six is sticks					
Seven is heaven					
Eight is a gate					
Nine is wine					
Ten is a hen					

Don't worry if you can't fill in all of the boxes in the table. Even if you can only think of one or two for each of them, that's fine.

Remember, while this may seem odd and even silly, the point is to connect memories in your brain to as many different brain areas as possible. All these different senses are based in different brain areas, and the more you use them, the more you use the incredible connecting power of your brain.

Just a couple of apparently silly associations with an imagined sensation can be the difference between something or someone being remembered or forgotten.

	Touch	Taste	Smell	Bodily sensation	Bodily movement
One is a bun	Sticky fingers	Sweet texture of raisins	Cinnamon	Sticking to roof of mouth	Chewing
Two is a shoe	Smooth leather		Sweat New leather Polish	Tightness round toes	Tying laces
Three is a tree	Rough bark	Cherry	Cherry blossom	Leaning against the trunk	Plucking a leaf
Four is a door	Brass door handle		Fresh varnish	Struck by door	Pulling open heavy door
Five is a hive	Bee on skin	Honey	Honey	Sting	Brushing away bee
Six is sticks	Rough wood in hands		Wood smoke	Splinter in finger	Chopping
Seven is heaven	Silken robes		Incense	Floating	Playing a harp
Eight is a gate	Metal catch		Newly oiled hinge	Sitting on swinging gate	Climbing onto gate
Nine is wine	Bottle	Red wine flavour	Red wine bouquet	Smoothly running down gullet	Pouring glass
Ten is a hen	Feathers	Chicken sandwich	Chicken roasting	Chicken piece in mouth	Biting chicken drumstick

These are just some examples – everyone forms different associations with these words. Any word can be linked to thousands of images and sensations, and when you combine words, you get millions of possible combinations.

And that's the strength of this technique. If you are trying to remember something it's important to make it really stand out in your mind. There is no better way of doing this than by making it *unique*. If you combine – say – the three senses of vision, bodily movement and taste, it is almost certain that you will come up with an image that you have never had before.

That image will in turn be linked to the person or thing you are trying to remember, and its uniqueness will give that memory a greater chance of survival in your mind.

So let's go back to the four people at the beginning of the chapter.

Peter's traumatic experience with Margaret had made him highly motivated to make sure he never forgets someone's name again. He had learned to make a slide show of the faces and names, and was now well-practised at adding a soundtrack.

When Peter met new people now, he not only ran the vision and sound parts of the multimedia show in his head, he also added at least one other channel. If he met a bald man, for instance, he would imagine how the smooth head would feel to the touch.

Simon added other channels to his sound and vision media show when studying for his exams. He would link lists of facts or procedures using the pegword method, and then would use various mixtures of vision, sound, smell, taste, touch and bodily movements and sensations to strengthen the memories.

Marion had no problem adding tastes, smells and bodily sensations/movements to the mental sounds and images of her books. She found that she got much more out of the novels while she was reading them, and also remembered them much better afterwards.

Joe didn't have any difficulty in making his shopping lists truly multimedia, by imagining the taste, smell and texture of the items he was to remember.

Make better use of words to improve your memory

Whether you are more of a verbaliser or a visualiser, almost everyone uses a bit of both when they are thinking and learning. To boost your memory to its maximum, you should use both types of thinking to the best of your ability.

Even if you find making mental images in the various senses difficult, it is well worth persevering with it as we know that people can become better at this with practice.

Test your memory

Read the following list of words, deciding whether each word begins with a vowel or a consonant. Read only once, close your eyes, and see how many you can remember.

Wall

Ostrich

Field

Bell

Slug

Soldier

Soil

Acre

Girl

Tree

How many did you get right? If you got them all after just one reading, that is pretty good indeed. Most people will have remembered only some of them.

Now read the second list of words below, this time deciding whether each word is living or non-living. Again, read the words just once and try to memorise them.

Floor

Sky

Turkey

Tower

Pilot

Worm

Grass

Man

Mile

Flower

How many did you get right this time?

You may have remembered more of the second list than the first. This is because making the judgment 'living versus non-living' forced you to do more mental processing over the meanings of the words than in the first list, where you simply had to make superficial judgments as to whether the words began with vowels or consonants.

By forcing your brain to penetrate into the meanings of the words to be learned, it automatically made a stronger memory trace for each word than when you didn't have to do this.

This is an example of *active reading,* and the same principles can apply to *active listening.* We remember what we *do* better than what we are *told,* and active reading/listening is an example of mental 'doing'.

By processing the information in books, newspapers, television, films, lectures or conversations in this way, you can greatly improve your memory – and you don't have to be a great visualiser to do so.

Categorising and organising

Language is one of the great achievements of the human brain. You can use your brain's language supercomputer to make remembering easier by *categorising* and *organising* the things you want to remember.

Here are some simple tips for keeping on the ball. The acronym here is BALL – which stands for:

- **B**ullet point
- **A**sk questions
- **L**ink to what you know already
- **L**ist into categories

Let's look at each of these in turn.

Bullet point your memory (BALL)

Most of the things we have to learn boil down to a few key facts, but we are often distracted by irrelevancies and clutter.

Journalists are taught to get down the essentials of a story – *who, what, when, where, how and why*. If you are reading an article, trying to follow assembly or operating instructions, watching a film or listening to a talk, you will remember more if you mentally bullet point the information.

Bullet points are like fence posts between which are slung the wires of memories. An advantage of reading is that you can skim the text first, picking out a few key points, before going over it again in detail. Making these points in your mind is a bit like going ahead and hammering in all the fence posts before you go back to string the wires.

Try this technique now with the following passage. Quickly skim through the piece to get the gist of it. Then, in the table below, write five to seven bullet points that sum up the piece.

1.	
2.	
3.	
4.	
5.	
6.	
7.	

CAN CREATIVITY BE TAUGHT?

Let's not beat about the bush – the answer to this question is a cautious and guarded 'yes'. When schoolchildren are exposed to teaching aimed at creative, divergent thinking, they score better in tests of creativity. What we don't know yet is whether or not this translates into tangible achievements when they leave school, however[28].

These are the conclusions of the eminent US cognitive scientist Professor Ray Nickerson of Tufts University. He believes that all of us have a huge untapped potential for being more creative, and he also argues that creativity is good for the quality of life of the individual, as well as for society. Shaking off old habits of thinking is, however, a key element in unlocking this potential.

Imagery is one way of shaking off these shackles, particularly where the problems you are facing are blue-sky, unfamiliar, and not amenable to deductive solutions. But problem solving may not be the key to creativity. Rather, finding the problem may be the key to creative breakthroughs in science, art, design and technology. In other words, 'What's the question?' may be an even more important challenge than, 'What's the answer?'

Let's look at the art students at a prestigious Chicago art school. The researchers followed up on the students years after they left to see how dealers, critics and gallery owners rated their creative success. When the researchers looked back at how the front-runners differed from the more modest achievers in the techniques and strategies they had used as students, clear differences popped up.

The students who became creative achievers tended to explore the subject they were painting to a greater extent — using all the senses. They felt it, sniffed it, held it up to the light, moved it, weighed it, and so on. They also chopped and changed their approach a lot. On the other hand, the artists who had not made it creatively more than a decade later would, as students, tend to pick a subject, look at it for a relatively short time, and then plough ahead with the work without making many changes.

It seemed, in other words, as if the creative artists were wrestling with establishing the right artistic question — they were thinking about the problem for a longer and more tortuous period than the less creative people. And they seemed to do this by deliberately trying to shake their brains out of well-worn tracks of mental habit by engaging all their senses in exploring the object.

Children who are taught to 'question the question' — that is, who do not accept the immediate definition of a problem, but explore different ways of defining it — become more creative in the longer term, it seems[29]. And imagery can help shake your mind out of the rut established by the obvious, in-your-face question.

The problem is, we tend to educate our children to meekly accept the problems posed for them, and to solve them in quite conventional, analytical ways. There can be little doubt that this is at a cost of stunting some non-analytical pathways where the challenge is to define the problem in new ways before it can be solved. Yet it doesn't take much to liberate young brains from these mind-habits. Take the following research with adolescent pupils in London schools, for instance[30].

This study looked at the effects of just one lesson, held once a fortnight, over a period of two years that began with several classes of 12 year olds. Though this was a science lesson, it was just as much a lesson in thinking, and in particular in finding problems and questions, as much as in solving them. In other words, these lessons were much more about teaching the children how to think than about teaching them specific scientific principles. This training in thinking improved their exam results across a number of subjects two years later.

Go back to page 173 and fill in the bullet points. Now, and with these bullet points in mind, read the passage again more carefully this time: you'll find that the details are easier to remember because you have the basics in mind already. After you've read it, you can then *test* yourself that you've remembered it by revising the bullet points without looking at the article, and filling in as many of the details as you can remember.

Simon used this technique when he was studying, and he used to combine it with his pegword method, strengthening the bullet points with images.

Peter would bullet point in his mind the information he gleaned from people at parties, and when he next met them would impress them with his memory of their backgrounds.

Marion didn't bullet point the chapters of the novels as she first read them – that would have spoiled their impact. But if she had read the book before, or if she was just going over it again before the book group, she would use the bullet point method to get the book clear in her mind.

Joe began to use bullet points to categorise his shopping lists – vegetables, cooking ingredients, household materials, fridge. These memory 'fence posts' made it easier to remember the details within each category.

The bullet points I picked out for the passage above are these:

1. Creativity can be taught.
2. Old thinking habits have to be shaken off.
3. Using mental images can help shake off these habits.
4. Key to creativity may be finding new questions more than finding new answers.
5. The best artists spend more time exploring their subject through various senses.
6. We teach children to solve problems that we give them, not to come up with new problems.
7. Teaching children new ways to think improves their exam results.

Ask questions of your memory (BALL)

You have skimmed the passage above and picked out a few bullet points. Before you read it again in detail, take a couple of seconds to bring to mind what you know about this subject. For instance, you might recall what you read about imagery and memory earlier in this chapter. Or you might think about your own school experiences, comparing teachers who did or didn't encourage you to think creatively.

Add these facts to your list of bullet points by writing them in the table below. Even assembling these few facts means your mind is better prepared to take in the new information you're reading.

List of extra bullet points from your own memory
1
2
3
4

You might like to try this with another article from a magazine or newspaper. Skim through it to find out what it's about, and then take a few seconds to dredge from your memory what you know already about the subject. Underline the bullet points from the article and then jot down the extra ones that you've pulled out of your memory.

Link to what you know already (BALL)

Now, as you read the passage on creativity, *link* what you are reading to the bullet points, trying to keep them in mind as you take in the details of the story. You can use the same method when watching a film or television programme, or listening to a lecture.

This is *active reading/listening* and is the verbal equivalent of learning by doing. Rather than passively receiving the information you want to remember, you are *acting on* the information with your mind by linking it to the bullet point 'fence posts' you knocked into your mental soil.

List into categories (BALL)

Another aspect of active reading or listening is to *organise* the information. Take the passage you have read twice now as an example. One part of your active reading technique that can help you remember it much better is to re-organise the passage in your own mind.

For example, you could gather together in your mind the parts that dealt with creativity and *education*, those covering creativity and *habit* and those related to creativity and *imagery*. In going over the article in your mind, putting your own structure to it, you will be guaranteed to remember it more clearly and for longer. I've copied the passage again below, putting these three themes in different fonts.

Can creativity be taught?

Let's not beat about the bush – the answer to this question is a cautious and guarded 'yes'. When schoolchildren are exposed to teaching aimed at creative, divergent thinking, they score better in tests of creativity. What we don't know yet is whether or not this translates into tangible achievements when they leave school, however. (education)

These are the conclusions of the eminent US cognitive scientist Professor Ray Nickerson of Tufts University. He believes that all of us have a huge untapped potential for being more creative, and he also argues that creativity is good for the quality of life of the individual, as well as for society. Shaking off old habits of thinking is, however, a key element in unlocking this potential. (habit)

Imagery is one way of shaking off these shackles, particularly where the problems you are facing are blue-sky, unfamiliar, and not amenable to deductive solutions. But problem solving may not be the key to creativity. Rather, finding the problem may be the key to creative break-throughs in science, art, design and technology. In other words, 'What's the question?' may be an even more important challenge than, 'What's the answer?' (imagery)

Let's look at the art students at a prestigious Chicago art school. The researchers followed up on the students years after they left to see how dealers, critics and gallery owners rated their creative success. When the researchers looked back at how the front-runners differed from the more modest achievers in the techniques and strategies they had used as students, clear differences popped up. (habit)

The students who became creative achievers tended to explore the subject they were painting to a greater extent – using all the senses. They felt it, sniffed it, held it up to the light, moved it, weighed it, and so on. They also chopped and changed their approach a lot. On the other hand, the artists who had not made it creatively more than a decade later would, as students, tend to pick a subject, look at it for a relatively short time, and then plough ahead with the work without making many changes. (imagery)

It seemed, in other words, as if the creative artists were wrestling with establishing the right artistic question – they were thinking about the problem for a longer and more tortuous period than the less creative people. And they seemed to do this by deliberately trying to shake their brains out of well-worn tracks of mental habit by engaging all their senses in exploring the object. (habit)

Children who are taught to 'question the question' – that is, who do not accept the immediate definition of a problem, but explore different ways of defining it – become more creative in the longer term, it seems. And imagery can help shake your mind out of the rut established by the obvious, in-your-face question. (education)

The problem is, we tend to educate our children to meekly accept the problems posed for them, and to solve them in quite conventional, analytical ways. There can be little doubt that this is at a cost of stunting some non-analytical pathways where the challenge is to define the problem in new ways before it can be solved. Yet it doesn't take much to liberate young brains from these mind-habits. Take the following research with adolescent pupils in London schools, for instance. (education)

This study looked at the effects of just one lesson, held once a fortnight, over a period of two years that began with several classes of 12 year olds. Though this was a science lesson, it was just as much a lesson in thinking, and in particular in finding problems and questions, as much as in solving them. In other words, these lessons were much more about teaching the children how to think than about teaching them specific scientific principles. For example, the children were presented with a group of different objects and instruments and rather than being asked to answer a question about these, they were asked to come up with some *questions* that could be asked of or with these objects. Similarly, they were asked to think about what different *dimensions* **these objects could be classified on – e.g. natural vs man-made; colour; weight; malleability; function, etc. This training in thinking improved their exam results across a number of subjects two years later. (education)**

There's nothing special about these categories, and it's clear that some of the text could be placed in more than one category. The important thing, however, is that you are learning by doing: mentally breaking up the text you are reading (or the film you are watching, or whatever) into your own categories, embedding it more firmly into your brain and so binding the information tighter into the existing network of connections.

Let's take another example. Suppose you have decided to take up a hobby such as bird watching and you are reading an article about a trip organised by your local bird watching group.

The article gives a day-by-day description of the various birds the group saw during the journey. One way of reading this article is simply to accept the author's presentation of the information – on Friday we saw this, Saturday that, and Sunday something else.

But active reading means that *you* choose how to organise the information – that is the different birds seen – irrespective of when they were seen. You can, for instance, make a few mental baskets – sea birds, marshland birds, hawks, small tree birds... and so on.

These do not have to be accurate ornithological categories – in fact it's better that they are your own idiosyncratic mental baskets. So, when you read '...we had a fantastic sighting of an Arctic tern early on Saturday morning,' you should be mentally noting 'Arctic tern – seabird,' at the same time.

Peter used this method when meeting new people – both socially and at work. He was better at remembering people's names, and was now seeing whether he could improve his memory for individual details about the subjects.

Peter had to meet scores of people every week in his job as a salesman. A retired colleague told him that remembering something about a client's family – their spouse's job, say, or what their child was studying – was crucial in building a good relationship with the client.

Now, when someone told Peter something about their family, he wouldn't just let that information stand as it was presented to him – he would pigeon-hole it.

If someone at a party said, 'My husband's an insurance broker,' Peter would mentally note 'financial services', putting that person into the same mental basket as the banker wife of one of his clients earlier that day.

The mere act of *organising* that piece of information by putting it in a category means that it is much more likely to be remembered.

To make the best of your memory, ideally you should use a combination of word- and image-based methods. For instance, you can pigeon-hole someone's job while at the same time making a mental picture of that job.

Both the category and image will help glue together memories from different people, places and facts that you have gleaned.

Make learning stick by testing yourself at longer intervals

Learning sticks when you use what you have learned – even occasionally. What you learn is seldom lost, though. Even if you can't recall something, it is easier to re-learn it if you've learnt it before.

Let's go back to Peter. Though his memory had improved by using a mixture of imagery and verbal methods, he wanted to make sure that when he met someone socially or at work weeks or months after he had first met them, he would remember their name.

You can help ensure this happens by pulling out these names from your memory every so often in the meantime. Suppose Peter met three new people today – Mary Simons, Keith McLean and Sue Brodie. He didn't know if or when he would meet them again, but for business reasons he wanted to make sure he remembered their names.

He used the slide show with soundtrack and other tips that I described earlier, but in addition he used the technique of *expanded rehearsal*. A few moments after he had memorised their names he *tested* himself by recalling the face-name pairs, along with those details he had stored in the slide show.

He then waited for a slightly longer time – roughly 30 seconds – and did this again. Two minutes later, he tested himself once more, and then again at a longer interval – 10 minutes, say. An hour later, he briefly recalled the names and faces, and then again three hours after. He tested himself again 12 hours later and then two days after that. After a week he would retrieve their names and faces whenever he had an odd moment, and again a month later.

He didn't have to worry about remembering the details of their lives that he had stored in his memory with his slide show and soundtrack. After recalling their names and faces on eight occasions over a month, these details stuck in his memory like confetti to a wet road.

One reason that the information you acquire while cramming for an exam doesn't stick is that in studying like that, you don't get much practice at pulling the learned facts out of your memory. The very act of retrieving them from the sticky spider's web of your memory gets them entangled in that web more firmly.

What's more, if you successfully recall them when they are beginning to weaken with time (hence the expanding time intervals between remembering them), this winds them even tighter into the web.

Simon found studying so much easier after he started using this test-yourself method in conjunction with the slide show and soundtrack techniques and making summaries of the material he had to learn. Rather than reading and memorising hour after hour in the evening, he would pick a topic, summarise it in a slide show, and test himself after two seconds, 10 seconds, 30 seconds, two minutes, 10 minutes, one hour ... and so on.

He did this whenever he had a free moment – waiting at a traffic light, walking down a corridor, or while sitting at his desk. It didn't take any more time – in fact, he found that he didn't have to spend nearly as long studying because this method used his memory so much more efficiently.

Marion found herself going over the plots, scenes, characters and themes of her beloved novels in this way. As a result, she now impresses her fellow book group members with her ability to relate aspects of the current book they are reading to books they had read months and even years before.

Joe began to take pride in being able to remember not just a few items of shopping, but also more complicated lists – such as screws, nails and other items for his do-it-yourself projects. He usually kept a backup list, but he tried not to use it, and found that both his memory and his confidence in his memory improved significantly.

Mix up your learning, don't max it.

There's a strange fact about learning: certain things that make it *easier* to remember in the *short term* actually make you *forget* more quickly in the *long term* and vice versa. What's going on here? The following box 'Why mixing is better than maxing' explains.

Let's go back to Joe. Joe was a methodical kind of guy. He liked to finish one thing before he started another. He also liked to get things right, and he simply had to pass his exams. That's why he would spend from shortly after dinner until midnight, reading and re-reading one topic of one subject, memorising his notes until he had them right.

Through experience, he found that he learned the stuff more quickly if he did that, rather than switching to a new topic or subject before he had mastered the first one.

What he didn't notice, though, was that while he learned *faster* in this way, the information didn't *stick* as well or for as long. He didn't find it easy to change his technique, but after working through this programme, he tried moving to a '*mix-it*' way of learning, as opposed to his old '*max-it*' strategy on one single topic.

Here's what he did: he would set aside a fixed time to

WHY MIXING IS BETTER THAN MAXING

'What does not kill me makes me stronger.' This famous comment by Nietzche applies not only to life, but also to memory. Plants that grow in greenhouses without experiencing the challenge and stress of the wind will snap in half if they face a strong wind when transplanted outside. Memories that are laid down without challenge are similarly fragile[31].

This is one reason why cramming your subject in one long grinding study session before an exam means your mind is blank of all that knowledge soon after the exam is over. The paradox is that you learn quicker when you focus on one subject and learn it by rote, but that learning doesn't last as long as when you mix it with other types of learning. It is better for a schoolchild to learn a bit of chemistry, then some maths, followed by some French, mixing up short sessions of learning, than spend hours and days on one subject. Of course, in the short term, you get lots of interference, and it can be frustrating because you are learning more slowly. But this learning is much more solidly based in your network of brain connections, not least because you are not only *storing* these memories, but also getting more practice at *retrieving* them from the thick forest of competing memories. And, like trees in a dense Amazonian forest that have to grow tall in the competition for light, so memories that are learnt under these more challenging circumstances also grow strong and longer-lasting.

study – say, two and a quarter hours, and would split this into eight 15-minute chunks, with a short break between each. To each of the periods he would assign a quite different topic from different subjects on his course.

He would take a small section of each topic and use his slide show, soundtrack and pegwords techniques to learn this information. This would take him five to 10 minutes. He would then test himself on this after two, 10, 30, 60 seconds, and five minutes.

While he was waiting to test himself, he would start preparing his slide show for the topic of the next 15-minute session. This ensured he wasn't sitting twiddling his thumbs waiting for the intervals between recall tests to pass. But it also helped to get his brain cells firing in different patterns in the intervals and so strengthened the memories of the first topic.

This was tough at first. Joe found that he muddled the topics, for instance getting one pegword list confused with another. But so long as he kept the chunks small and manageable, and was very systematic and disciplined when 'mixing it', he found that – just as the research has proved – two months later at the exams he remembered the mix-it material much better than the max-it stuff.

Marion experimented with keeping two books going, rather than her usual one. In the short term, she got a bit muddled between the names, plots and scenes, but as she learned to use the expanded rehearsal method (second… minute…hour…day…week), she found that novels didn't disappear into a blur the way they used to. Months later, she could remember plots and scenes that previously would have vanished from her memory.

Peter became renowned among clients and acquaintances for his memory for names, faces and personal details. He began to enjoy memorising this information, and found that both his social and work life benefited.

When Peter met someone new, he would make his now

habitual slide show with soundtrack. If he met a group of people, he would use other tricks, such as the various pegword methods.

To make sure the names and faces stuck, he would revise some of the names he had learned at odd moments during the day, whether stuck in a traffic jam or waiting for a client to arrive. He made sure he mixed the different people that he had memorised at different times and was careful not to keep revising the same – usually most recent – list.

Start working on your memory

Putting these memory methods into practice isn't difficult. The hard part is putting aside the time to do it. These tricks will only be of benefit after you have practised them, so it is easy to get discouraged because they seem to be harder work than your normal way of learning.

But research shows that if you persevere with methods like these, and really work at challenging your memory, then your memory will improve.

Set your first memory goals

The best way to start is to focus on one or two areas where you would really like to improve your memory. Common ones are names and faces, but there are many more. Choose one or two areas from the list below.

- ☀ Names and faces
- ☀ Non-fiction reading, including newspapers
- ☀ Fiction reading
- ☀ Films and television
- ☀ Jokes, stories, poetry or quotations

💡 Sporting facts
💡 Songs
💡 Games (cards and chess for example)
💡 Hobbies
💡 Financial markets
💡 History
💡 Politics
💡 Religion
💡 Weather
💡 Countryside and wildlife
💡 Science
💡 Geography
💡 Biographies
💡 Other

If your work or leisure interests do not involve meeting new people you might give a low priority to improving your ability to remember names and faces.

If you are interested in the countryside, however, you might like to improve your memory for different types of trees, flowers or fungi.

If you are interested in mechanical things, you might want to become more knowledgeable about vintage motor bikes or cars. It really doesn't matter what you decide to focus on first – the important thing is that you choose an area where you are *motivated* to use your memory more effectively.

If you have difficulty with people's names and faces, however, this can be a good one to start with if you are in contact with more than a small group of people. People really appreciate it when you remember details such as their name, and even more if you remember the name of their child or partner. The positive response you get from them can be very rewarding and encourage you to persist with your memory training.

'I can never remember any jokes.' How often have you heard someone say this? Jokes and interesting anecdotes can be another very rewarding area to sharpen your memory on. People like to be entertained and you will become rewarded and motivated if you manage to remember interesting or funny things you have heard, watched or read.

Write your first two main memory goals in the figure below. A goal might be something like remembering the names of the next 10/20/30 people you meet. Or remembering the name of at least one family member of 10 acquaintances. You might decide to try to remember a certain number of jokes or anecdotes. The possibilities are endless. The important thing is that you set yourself a clear memory goal.

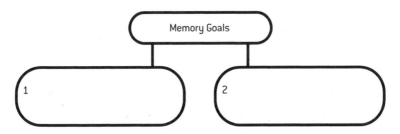

Choose your favourite memory strategies

There are several different memory strategies described in this chapter that you can use. Over time you may learn to use some, many or even all of them. But it is important that you choose at most one, two or three at first. You can then practise them thoroughly on your first memory goals. In that way, you are less likely to become discouraged and to give up before you see the benefits of your training.

Below is a list of all the memory strategies that I have described. Read through them and choose one, two or three that you plan to work on first.

ᵔᵔ Slide show
ᵔᵔ Method of loci
ᵔᵔ Pegword
ᵔᵔ Multimedia (using other senses)
ᵔᵔ BALL method
ᵔᵔ Expanded rehearsal (test at increasing intervals)
ᵔᵔ Mixing not maxing your learning

Now write your top three strategies in the chart:

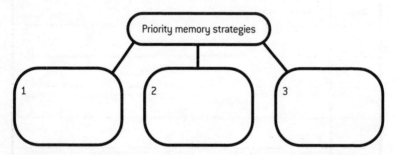

Start with number one and apply this to your first memory goal. Don't be over-ambitious in setting a date to achieve this goal. You will find it hard at first and progressively easier as you learn more and more. You can choose the time interval, but let's say arbitrarily that you will achieve your first memory goal in a week. After a week, return to the table below, and test yourself from memory on the material you decided you would learn.

GOAL 1 ITEMS	INFORMATION LEARNED (Test yourself from memory)
1	
2	
3	
4	
5	
6	
7	
8	
9	
10	
11	
12	
13	
14	
15	
16	
17	
18	
19	
20	

Don't worry if you don't manage to achieve it on the first test. Practise for another couple of days and then test yourself again. Once you have achieved your first memory goal, go on to the second one.

Spend the period of time you think is reasonable – say a week – and do the same for your second memory goal. Then test yourself in the table below.

GOAL 2 ITEMS	INFORMATION LEARNED (Test yourself from memory)
1	
2	
3	
4	
5	
6	
7	
8	
9	
10	
11	
12	
13	
14	
15	
16	
17	
18	
19	
20	

Only when you have got this correct from memory, go ahead with your third memory goal and test yourself again as before:

GOAL 3 ITEMS	INFORMATION LEARNED (Test yourself from memory)
1	
2	
3	
4	
5	
6	
7	
8	
9	
10	
11	
12	
13	
14	
15	
16	
17	
18	
19	
20	

Come back to these pages every time you think you have achieved your goal. Once you have achieved all three goals, review the strategies you have been using. In the following table, tick the strategies you have tried and then rate how useful you found them.

Strategy	Did you practise it fully?	If so, how useful did you find it: * = very little use ** = quite useful *** = very useful
Slide show		
Method of loci		
Pegword		
Multimedia (using other senses)		
BALL method		
Expanded rehearsal (test at increasing intervals)		
Mixing not maxing your learning		

Don't give up on a strategy unless you have given it a really good chance and tried it several times a day for at least a week: 50 times in total would be a good trial. If, after that, you decide that you should change strategies, try one of the other methods. Even if you have found the strategies you tried already to be very useful, it is worthwhile practising some of the other techniques that you haven't yet tried.

Choose two new memory goals and three strategies (which can be the same or different from your first ones) and write them in the boxes below.

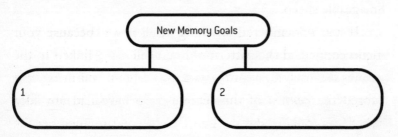

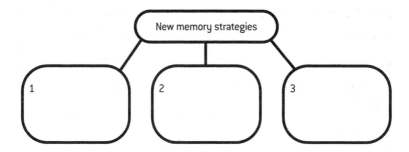

You should find that the more you practise learning, the easier it becomes. You might decide to extend your goals and become more ambitious. But it's important that you occasionally recall information that you learnt some time ago: successfully retrieving memories is the best way of tying them firmly into your brain.

Memories are, however, only as strong as the attention we give to them. Let's turn to the question of attention and concentration.

Test your memory

Earlier in this chapter, I asked you to remember two short passages of prose. One was about cows, the other about sheep. Try to remember as much as you can of each.

You would probably have remembered some of the text – probably more about the highly visualisable cows than the less imageable sheep.

If you remembered anything at all it was because your brain connected the pattern of brain cell firing linked to the stories themselves, with the pattern of brain cell firing that stored the *context* of this learning. To have had any idea what I was talking about when I asked you to remember the exercise, you had to re-create from memory the situation where and when you were reading this chapter, be it minutes, hours or days ago.

If your brain had stored none of this context, then my request that you remember doing the story learning exercise would not make sense. What I was doing was giving your brain a few clues about the context ('Earlier in the chapter I asked you to remember two short passages of prose'), and with these fragments your brain managed to re-create the moment when you were learning them.

Only once it had re-constructed this context could your brain pick out the information that was learnt in that context – the swinging udders of the cows, and the darting rat. These words and images triggered a distinct pattern of firing in the millions of onion-like cells throughout your brain – probably many more brain cells than the sheep story triggered.

At the same time, the context (me reading a book in bed half an hour ago, for instance) had triggered another unique pattern of brain-cell firing. So we have two vast pulses of activation spreading through your brain as you learnt the two stories – one for their content and another for the context in which you were learning them.

The key to memory – and to your being able to improve your memory – hangs on the brain's central trick of binding together these two sets of memories. A brain cell fires when it gets enough of a push from the axons of other brain cells itching and nagging at its surface.

Now, as all this happens, cells that don't have all that much to do with each other end up firing off at more or less the same time. This is not because they have always been wired up together, but simply because both happened to be triggered by the same cascade of activity in the brain – that is the surge of electrical activity generated by your learning the stories, as well as the activity triggered by the context.

It's a bit like being stuck in a delayed train with someone: at first you may not speak to them, but after an hour or two you will both be groaning and complaining together. A similar thing happens to brain cells. After a few repetitions of firing together, they tend to team up. When two connected neurons are triggered at the same time on several occasions, the cells and synapses between them change. When one fires now, it will pack a much bigger punch in triggering the other.

In other words, they become partners and in future will fire off in tandem much more readily than before. This is called 'Hebbian learning', named after the Canadian psychologist, Donald Hebb. The chemical change in cells and synapses is called 'long-term potentiation' (LTP).

So, as you learned the stories, the brain cells that registered the words and images of the stories themselves fired at the same time as the brain cells that registered the context of your learning them. And, hey presto, because they were all firing at the same time, you got these two waves of brain cell activity connected on the basis that cells that fire together, wire together.

When I asked you later to remember the stories you learnt, the context brain cells that I triggered by my request nudged awake their new sister brain cells registering the story content of udders, cows and sheep.

As we live our lives, experience gradually re-moulds us. Connections in the brain are made, and connections broken.

We learn and we forget. Anger transmutes to guilt, affection to resentment, despair to hope. You sign up for French classes and embark on re-moulding a few million brain cell connections as you wrestle with the grammar, vocabulary and pronunciation. But somehow you are too busy to continue and the connections wither.

Go to France on holiday next year, however, and you will be surprised by what slips from your lips as you relax over a glass of Chablis. Words and phrases you thought you had forgotten pop out. You even understand snatches of conversation between the two Frenchmen at the next table. Traces of those evening classes have lingered in your brain, filigreed into the trembling web of connections between brain cells.

Like the handsome prince in *Sleeping Beauty*, the sound of the French language on your holiday awakened those dormant connections, which still remained, unnoticed in the vast web of brain connections. There, in the chemistry of the synapses, the memory still lingered.

Nor do you forget the smell of new-baked bread from the bakery in the small French town where you had a wonderful holiday; the feeling of holding your first child for the first time; the moment you heard terrible news... Some experiences echo so widely and strongly through the brain that the changes in the connections they cause can never be undone.

Memories, then, are formed when brain cells become linked through firing together – *cells that fire together, wire together*. And once cells become embroidered together in this way – firing in concert – they become a secret brotherhood of remembrance. Solidarity is the essence of any brotherhood – one for all and all for one.

OH DON'T TELL ME THAT STORY *AGAIN*

'Oh not that story again, Dad!' Sound familiar? If not said to you, then perhaps said by you to your father, mother or grandfather? What *is* it about getting older that makes us retell the same stories with the twinkling-eyed conviction that our listeners will be riveted and amused, not having heard them before?

The leading cognitive psychologist Larry Jacoby, of Washington University at St Louis, has an answer. When we tell an anecdote or retrieve a memory, there are two quite different forces at play in our brains. The first is the sheer raw *familiarity* of the tale that has built up over many retellings. This familiarity makes the memory surface all too easily in our consciousness, and hence be told. Rallied against this momentum is the rapier of *recall*, and in particular the recall of *when, where* and *under what circumstances* you actually learned this story or fact. If you manage to remember that you told the story to the same group of people at a particular party in Geoff's house last spring, then the chances are that you will not let its familiarity force the story onto your lips. Such recall depends on a well-functioning set of frontal lobes. The good news is that older people can be trained to sharpen up this rapier and to learn to use recall more effectively to help us distinguish the apparently new from the truly new. Professor Jacoby and his colleagues showed that by gradually extending the length of time over which you recall familiar words that could all too easily be mistaken for new information, you can improve memory and reduce repetitive behaviour.

This Hebbian solidarity means that if one cell reacts, then its brother-cell will react too – the brotherhood of cells develops a group mind: it just needs one to act to trigger all the others into action. It is because of this 'all for one, one for all' welding of cellular souls that you can remember the stories you learnt by a few clues about the context that I fed you.

The secret of how to improve your memory should be becoming clear now. The bigger the brotherhood of cells that the memory is linked into, the more likely it is that you'll remember it later. One easy way to recruit millions of new members to this brotherhood is to link images in all the senses – sight, sound, touch, movement, taste – with whatever it is you have to remember, be it faces, facts, formulae, figures or files.

Remembering your wine

Are you a wine connoisseur, or are you an amateur oblivious of the finer nuances of the grape? Do friends who fancy themselves as cognoscenti after a couple of glasses browbeat you with loquacious reflections on the audacious gooseberries, oak-tainted butter and mellow jam that fill their mouths? Do you tend to stay mum and just drink?

If you do, then take heart. Unless they are true wine experts – and there are few of them around – if they talk while they taste they will snuff out their brain's ability to tell wines apart![32]

This was demonstrated in a simple study. A mixed group of wine experts and amateurs were asked to taste a wine, and then either talk about the taste, or speak about something irrelevant. They were then given three different wines, and had to say which one they had tasted a little while before.

While the experts did well no matter whether they had talked about the wine or about their gardens, the amateurs who had been talking about its taste and quality couldn't remember the first wine properly. If they were talking about something else, on the other hand, then they could remember which wine they had tasted.

So, the next time you are irritated by someone's amateur musings about the quality of your wine, just tell them that unless they shut up, they might as well be drinking sugary anti-freeze, for all their brains will be able to tell the difference!

Yes, if we rely too much on words in our contact with the world, we really do cut ourselves off from certain more immediate experiences and the skills and benefits they can produce. But it isn't just in memory for taste that it is impor-tant to free up and use our mind's eye, mind's palate and so on – it's also true for that most essential of day-to-day survival skills – learning.

We must use both words and images to make the most of our memory, however. I suggest you read over this chapter a few more times, until you have chosen the memory-sharpening methods that best suit your unique brain. In between readings remember to *practice* – you will not boost your memory unless you *practice* at least one or two of the techniques.

Let's turn now to the last and perhaps most important step of the programme – managing your mind.

Step 10:
Manage Your Mind

'Now where did I leave my glasses...?'

Catherine's office was a mess. As unpaid manager of the small charity, she worked long hours and found it quite stressful. She felt over-pressed, with a sense of always leaving things half-finished because some more pressing task cropped up. Catherine was always rushing, telling people how busy she was. The other volunteers wondered how on earth the charity could continue if Catherine left.

At the management committee meetings, the members made allowances for Catherine when she didn't have the agenda or minutes ready. They tolerated it when she deviated from the point and engaged in long, sometimes rambling, accounts of her experiences and difficulties. Catherine herself realised that she got sidetracked sometimes, but she had always been a bit 'scatty', though she was regarded as dedicated and well-meaning. As she has got older, her scattiness has got worse.

Catherine's concentration wasn't that good either, she realised. Even when the minutes were finished on time, they were full of errors because she was very poor at proofreading and her concentration easily lapsed when doing boring tasks.

When Catherine left the signed annual accounts for the charity behind on the train when she was on her way to the annual general meeting, which was to be attended by several important businessmen and potential donors, the committee became less tolerant and forgiving. After a stressful encounter, Catherine resigned and a new manager was appointed.

The committee were concerned that the new person would find the position as stressful as Catherine had. After a few weeks, however, they noticed that Celine, a recently retired teacher, managed to do the job in just a few mornings per week, instead of the six long days per week that Catherine had worked. The minutes were accurate and on time, and the board meetings took a fraction of the time that they had under Catherine.

How well do you manage your mind?

Are you a Catherine or a Celine? Are you forgetful and disorganised, or are you on the ball? Most of us are somewhere in between. Answer these questions:

Do you find yourself 'dithering', oscillating between one thing and another, not sure which one to do first?

A lot ☐ Sometimes ☐ Hardly ever ☐

Do you start to do something and then forget what it was that you intended to do?

A lot ☐ Sometimes ☐ Hardly ever ☐

Do you send an email saying you are attaching a document and then forget to do so?

A lot ❑   Sometimes ❑   Hardly ever ❑

Do you search everywhere for your spectacles only to find that they are in your pocket or on your forehead?

A lot ❑   Sometimes ❑   Hardly ever ❑

Do you find that your eyes have been moving over the page but that your mind hasn't been taking in what you're reading?

A lot ❑   Sometimes ❑   Hardly ever ❑

Do you start listening to the weather forecast for your part of the country, but find that by the time the forecaster gets to it your mind has wandered so that you miss what is said?

A lot ❑   Sometimes ❑   Hardly ever ❑

Do you look for something on a desk or in a drawer, only to find that it was right under your nose all the time?.

A lot ❑   Sometimes ❑   Hardly ever ❑

Do you throw away the thing you meant to keep and keep the thing you meant to throw away?

A lot ❑   Sometimes ❑   Hardly ever ❑

When you're introduced to someone, do you find that you haven't listened to the name and so can't remember it only seconds after you've been told?   A lot ❑   Sometimes ❑   Hardly ever ❑

Do you put things down and then not find them afterwards?

A lot ❑   Sometimes ❑   Hardly ever ❑

Give yourself two points for each 'A lot', one point for each 'Sometimes' and nought for each 'Hardly ever'. Now add up your scores.

15-20: You are a bit like Catherine, prone to being absent-minded and disorganised. You may have been like this most of your life, or perhaps you are going through a period of stress. It could be that you are a sort of 'absent-minded professor'. You have great things on your mind and so you don't pay attention to everyday things. If it is not a reaction to a period of stress or to preoccupation, this absent-mindedness probably causes you some stress in your life, as it did for Catherine. It also probably means that you get less done than you would like to.

7-14: Though perhaps not as extreme as Catherine, you are prone to absent-mindedness and inefficiency. You may look at other people who are less absent-minded and wonder how they achieve so much more than you. Sometimes you can be stressed by the difficulty you have in coping with a number of different demands on your time.

0-6: You are pretty well-organised and not particularly absent-minded, though you can make small slips at times.

If you scored over six in this test, you are not managing your mind as well as you might. The box below, 'The mind's general manager', explains what 'managing your mind' means, and why it is that some of us don't manage it as well as we might.

Some of us are born with a propensity to be absent-minded. This problem is made worse if we don't learn good habits of mental management. My own research has shown[32] that no matter what the cause of your absent-mindedness, it

THE MIND'S GENERAL MANAGER

It is not really surprising that the most complex object in the universe – the human brain – requires management. Without management, how can we navigate through the millions of different streams of information that hit our senses, and link these to the millions of different responses we might make?

Look at children. We have the most elaborate set of rules and institutions to protect children from themselves – to stop them being run over, to prevent them getting into trouble with the police, to make sure they don't damage their health by eating the wrong food... and so it goes on.

Our brain's general manager does what managers the world over do: it *sets* strategic goals and a corresponding group of tactical sub-goals. Then it checks – *monitors* – whether the goals are being met, and detects *errors* in what's being done. It also *corrects* errors and, if necessary, stops – *inhibits* – this from happening again.

Our frontal lobes carry out many of these managerial functions, but our brains are so complicated that they never do this perfectly, and that is why human beings are prone to errors and, at times, being disorganised. All these different functions of management are linked to different parts of the frontal lobes. And this part of the brain is not fully functioning and in place until we are in our early twenties. This is why young drivers are such bad insurance risks – *foresight* and *self-control* are also key functions of the frontal lobes.

Like any high-performance, thoroughbred machine, the frontal lobes can need retuning, or may never have been properly tuned in the first place. They can also be affected by stress, alcohol or distraction. And our frontal lobes are the part of the brain most vulnerable to the effects of ageing. So, the next time you say to yourself *'Where did I put my keys?'* just think of it as your frontal lobes not having *set* what you were supposed to be doing when you put the keys down and not *monitoring* whether you had noted the spot.

is often possible to become less absent-minded by learning habits of good mental management.

Why do I need to manage my mind better?

If your current way of life makes absolutely no demands on you and you are totally happy and contented, then you may not care about managing your mind better. But if that is the case, then it is likely that you are not building in much challenge, change and learning in your life either, and these are important factors if you want to stay sharp over the next couple of decades.

Assuming that you are actively engaged in activities that challenge you mentally, and assuming that you do not have near-perfect mental organisation already, it makes sense to start tuning up your brain's general manager so that you manage your mind more efficiently.

Any task you do that is not a well-ingrained habit can be improved if you use your mind manager to its full capacity. Whether it is reading a book or newspaper, listening to music, watching a film or television programme, having a conversation, assembling a piece of furniture, reading a timetable or planning a holiday – you can learn, enjoy and achieve more by tuning up your mind manager.

Let's look at ways you can train up your mind manager in key practical areas of your life.

Boost your memory by managing your mind

In the last chapter I outlined how you can improve your memory by using a number of methods to link new information to the knowledge you already have. One of these methods was BALL (Bullet point, Ask questions, List and Link). This helps you to read and listen actively by picking out the key points and linking them to what you know.

Doing this, however, assumes that you are paying attention to what you are reading or hearing, and what's more, that you are concentrating on the key points. We have all had the experience of reading and only realising afterwards that we haven't been taking in what's on the page. This is because our frontal lobes have not kept our attention on the task in hand. This also happens in conversations, lectures or films, when the mind drifts.

But this mind-managing part of your brain can do a lot more than just keep your mind focused on the subject in hand: it can also help you absorb the information strategically and intelligently so that you learn and remember much more of what you are reading, hearing or watching.

It can, for instance, help you to make the most of your mental abilities by checking the following every so often while you are reading, watching or listening:

☀ Am I taking this in?
☀ What's the reason I'm reading/watching/listening to this?
☀ Can I see the wood for the trees?
☀ Am I keeping the main argument in mind?
☀ Am I avoiding being sidetracked to other issues?

Practise mind management

In addition to the BALL method there is something else you must learn to do routinely while reading or listening:

- ☀ *pause* from time to time, then
- ☀ *pose the question* – am I taking this in?
- ☀ *put into words* – say what your goal is.

Learning to *pause* is the single most important thing you can learn in mind management. When you read, watch or listen, your attention tends to become absorbed in the material. But this absorption can mean that you lose track of other things, for instance:

- ☀ what information you want from the material,
- ☀ whether or not you are actually taking in what you are reading,
- ☀ whether there's something else you should be doing,
- ☀ whether or not you are using active reading/memory strategies as you read.

Learn to PAUSE

Pausing is as simple as it sounds, but it's harder to do in the middle of mind-engrossing activities than it appears. It's easy to remember to *pause* when that's what you are thinking about, but the whole point about pausing is to be able to do it in the middle of the hurly-burly of attention-consuming activities.

Take cooking, for instance. If you are following a recipe that involves several different activities, it is easy to become engrossed in – say – preparing the vegetables, while forgetting to check whether the sauce is burning.

This is because your attention becomes locked into the vegetable task, and your mind doesn't manage your attention well enough to leave some spare capacity for checking whether you are doing all the things you should be doing.

How can you avoid burning the sauce? By learning a simple mental habit. That habit is to routinely break into tasks, to stop what you are doing, and to give your mind manager a chance to check that everything is on course. In other words, you learn to PAUSE.

It can help if you choose one or two catchphrases that you link with pausing, such as:

'Hold on.'
'Stop for a moment.'
'Let's see.'
'Take five.'

Choose one or more catch phrase that you might use: write them in the box below.

1	
2	
3	

Shortly, you will be able to practise this technique with a piece of text. Every time there is a new paragraph, just pause for a couple of seconds, using your PAUSE catch phrase.

Learn to POSE the question

If you manage to break off from the task or activity with the help of your catch phrase, it helps to POSE yourself questions like:

- What am I meant to be doing?
- Am I taking this in?
- Is this relevant?
- Am I forgetting something?
- Have I gone off track?
- Where should I be focusing?
- Is there anything else I should be thinking about?
- Do I need to remember this?
- Is this important?
- Am I concentrating enough?
- Am I giving this more attention than it deserves?
- Is there anything I've forgotten?

Often just remembering to pause will bring questions like this to mind. But it helps if you can learn the habit of both PAUSING and POSING a number of different questions to yourself.

This doesn't just apply to reading – it applies to everything from doing your housework to meeting the bank manager, or from programming a DVD recorder to writing a letter.

Learn to PUT into words

The easiest way to make sure you don't get absent-mindedly sidetracked from what you want to do is to PUT into words what you are aiming at.

It's probably best to say these words inside your head rather than out loud. But when it's something important, you often hear people talking themselves through what they should be doing.

If you are prone to absent-mindedness, or if you have a number of things you have to do at the same time, this type of internal commentary – PUT-ting the task into words – is a big help to your mind manager. The jargon for this is *metacognition* – literally thinking about thinking. Here are examples of metacognitive self-talk:

- ·☀· Hold on, I'm getting distracted here.
- ·☀· I'm losing focus – need to be more alert.
- ·☀· I'm getting too agitated – must calm down and think about what I need to do.
- ·☀· I'll break this down – first I have to do x, then y, then…

Good police drivers talk themselves through their own mental states as much as they talk themselves through what's happening on the road.

I'll take you through some simple exercises so that you can try this out. But you also have to put in plenty of practice in your own everyday activities.

The best mind managers apply this to all areas of their lives. To make the most of your brain's huge and partly untapped capacity, you must learn to manage its resources better. My research has shown that if you learn these three mental habits, you will boost your mental abilities and stay really sharp[33].

☼ *PAUSE*
☼ *POSE* the Question
☼ *PUT* into Words

The box below, 'Why policemen talk to themselves', explains why it helps to PUT what you are doing into words. You manage your mind better and avoid mistakes and mental disorganisation.

Try mind management while reading

Read the following passage. After every paragraph, this symbol appears – ♦ – meaning *PAUSE*. Whenever you see it,

WHY POLICEMEN TALK TO THEMSELVES

Police drivers are sometimes trained to give a running commentary to themselves about what they are seeing and doing as they drive. The internal commentary might sound something like this:

Car on side road to left ... looks like he might pull out ... slow down ... clear road ahead ... line of cars approaching, behind slow truck ... car might pull out into this lane ... road surface dry, clear ahead ... can speed up ... no hurry though, so may as well keep within speed limit ... hold on, that car coming up looks like he's way over the limit ... where can I turn? Busy road, take care as I pull in here

... not sure I'm as alert as I should be – better stop for a coffee – stay focused ...

The left frontal lobe of your brain – located above your left eye – is key to *setting* what you are aiming at, and *re-setting* what you are doing when you drift off task. This part of the brain is closely linked with the speech and language centres in the left half of your brain.

PUT-ting into words what he is doing and noticing helps a policeman's mind manager to stay focused and on task. It also means that he notices things earlier than he would if he were not managing his attention in this way.

The Russian psychologist Vygotsky believed that, as young children, we learn to control our behaviour, thoughts and emotions by this type of talking to ourselves. He described a young child's monologues as she played with dolls, something like this ... *'I'll tidy these away – good girl ... oh look, you've made a mess, that was naughty ... Now don't cry, mummy will clear it up...'*

Vygotsky argued that young children start out by being first physically, then verbally, guided by adults – instructed what to do and when. Gradually they make these adults' words and phrases their own, speaking them out loud at first like the little girl with her dolls, then gradually only inside their heads.

As adults we steer our way through the temptations, stresses, demands and pleasures of life and work through an intricate internal monologue of self-talk – admonitions, encouragements, warnings and hopes. Without these, we would not be able to pass exams, hold down jobs, pay mortgages and cope with all the complexities of the world. And, of course, some people don't.

take a couple of seconds to check whether you were taking in what you were reading in the previous paragraph. You might also **POSE** the question, 'Am I taking this in?' or 'What's the main point of that paragraph?'

Albert Einstein was one of a number of scientists from the German-language tradition who revolutionised scientific think-ing in the 20th century – surely one of the great communal acts of creation of the human mind. Was it a mere coincidence that the prevailing philosophy of German science and education at the turn of the century emphasised the importance of visual imagery in science and engineering? ♦

Einstein attended the Canton school in Aarau, Switzerland, which was set up by followers of the Swiss education pioneer Johann Pestalozzi. In his book 'Insights of Genius', the science historian Arthur Miller, of University College, London, pinpoints this influ-ence as central to Einstein's intellectual development. To Pestalozzi, imagery was the foundation of all knowledge, and visual thinking a fundamental and powerful feature of the mind. ♦

According to this view, artists and scientists re-create the world by making images, and indeed Einstein himself realised that his own mode for creative thinking was visual imagery. In 1895, at the age of 16, while still at school in Switzerland, Einstein used visual imagery to create one of the fundamental thought experi-ments of turn-of-the-century physics, an experiment in imagery that led to the conclusion that the speed of light is always constant, irrespective of any relative movement between the observer and the source of light. ♦

The 16 year old's experiment visualised a cart in which the observer sits, chasing a point on a light wave. The assumption of Newtonian physics was that as the cart reached the speed of the point of light, it would be as if two trains were travelling at the same high speed: to passengers on the two trains looking at each other through the windows, it would seem that the two trains were not moving relative to each other. ♦

If this were true of the point of light on the light wave, however, Einstein visualised that the observer on the cart would see just the point of light bobbing up and down like a cork on the wave, and not moving forward at all. ♦

On the basis of the intuition born of this visual image – a point on a light wave bobbing up and down and not moving forward relative to a scientist careering along on a cart beside it at the same speed – Einstein immediately rejected the Newtonian option. Visual imagery made him conclude that the speed of light (in a vacuum) is constant – eternally c – irrespective of how fast the light's watcher is travelling. And, it turns out, he was right. ♦

Of course, it is only a hypothesis that the visual-imagery dominated ethos of his school and of the German scientific world of that time was responsible for this fundamental insight. Einstein was a genius, and may well have come up with that insight even without such an education. But the fact is that Einstein himself declared visual imagery to be fundamental to his scientific thinking. ♦

Einstein went so far as to say that 'words or language ... do not seem to play any role in my mechanism of thought'. Rather, he said, 'my elements of thought are ... images ...' [34] ◆

Perhaps the most famous example of visual imagery underlying an act of scientific creative thinking is a dream of the great scientist Kekule that led to the discovery of the structure of the benzene ring. Dozing by the fire, Kekule saw atoms gambolling in his mind's eye. Then they joined into long strings, twisting like snakes. Suddenly, he noticed one of the snakes seize hold of its own tail. In a flash he awoke: this visual image had unlocked one of the great scientific puzzles of the day – that the benzene molecule had a ring structure. ◆

HOW THE MIND MANAGER
IMPROVES YOUR READING SKILLS

You read a Shakespeare sonnet differently from the way you read the minutes of the governing body of a charity. If you don't use your mind manager to read, you may well plod through each one word for word, in much the same way. The result will be that you won't get what you want out of either text.

Why is this? You read the sonnet for the pleasure and beauty of the language, so you read it slowly, and probably re-read many of the lines. You may stop to conjure up the images linked to the text and you may read it aloud at times to get the music of the words.

Unless you are the chairman or secretary of the meeting, you probably don't want to proofread the minutes, and so your job is to read them solely to judge how accurately they represent the discussions and decisions of the meeting. What's more, you are probably more concerned about some issues than others, and will want to give extra thought and attention to those points while you are reading them.

For example, you will probably skim over the list of the attendees and the discussion about the location and format of the staff party. But you will want to very carefully read the summary of the report you gave as chair of the finance sub-committee.

Now this may sound very easy and obvious. But the problem is this: *once you start reading, it is very easy to lose track of these obvious things.* That brings us to the nub of what the mind manager does: it hovers above what you are doing, not letting your mind get so completely absorbed that it goes off track.

When you drive away from your house to go on holiday for two weeks with no idea whether or not the heating is off it is because your mind was absent when you carried out the task of switching off the heating. This, in turn, was because your mind manager didn't over-ride the routine adjustment of the central heating and bring it into awareness. Neither did it keep in mind that you were about to go on holiday, and that this particular adjustment of the central heating was especially important.

This is what absent-mindedness is all about – not consciously attending to what you are doing at this moment. It is also about keeping half a mental eye on the bigger picture. For example, you don't have to read every word of every section of the committee minutes, but only those sections that are important.

The mind manager keeps in mind what's important *while* you are reading.

Try mind management in everyday life

If you try nothing else in the mind management scheme, try to practise *PAUSE* every so often.

If it helps, you can use the symbol ♦ to represent *PAUSE* in your mind's eye.

You might like to try setting your watch or phone to beep at regular intervals, and use that alert sound to remind you to defocus from what you're concentrating on and *POSE* questions like, *'Am I on track?', 'Am I doing what I set out to do?'*

You can also use natural breaks or events to trigger a *PAUSE* ♦. The end of a paragraph is one example of this. Here are some other examples:

- ⟨ϙ⟩ Whenever you check the recipe book while cooking, use this as a chance to *PAUSE.*
- ⟨ϙ⟩ If you are following instructions to assemble a piece of furniture or programme an electronic device, *PAUSE* whenever you look at a different diagram in the instructions.
- ⟨ϙ⟩ Whenever you get up out of a chair or walk into a different room, *PAUSE* and *POSE* the question: *'Is there anything I've forgotten?'*
- ⟨ϙ⟩ If you are taking part in a meeting, whether as a chairman, secretary or member, *PAUSE* whenever a new person speaks. *POSE* the questions:
  - *Are we sticking to the agenda?*
  - *Is what I am thinking of saying relevant to the main point of discussion?*
  - *Are we being sidetracked?*
- ⟨ϙ⟩ If you are talking to someone – for example, a work

colleague, a builder discussing an extension to your house or a financial adviser discussing your investments, *PAUSE* whenever – for instance – the person asks you a question. *POSE* the questions:

- *What is the goal of this meeting?*
- *What are the sub-goals to get there?*
- *Where have we got to?*
- *What's the next step?*

No matter how old you are, you still have the most complex machine in the universe inside your skull. But to make the most of its immense powers, you have to manage it well. This mind management programme will help you do this, but like most of the other exercises in this book, you need to practise in order to give it a chance. Good luck!

Finale:
Make the Most of Your Prime of Life

Let's make it absolutely clear: you have the chance to make yourself mentally younger if you put into practice at least some of the 10 steps in this programme. The scientific evidence is clear: *challenge, change, learning, exercise, diet, stimulation, controlling stress, mental activity, memory training and mind management* can all greatly improve your mental sharpness no matter how old you are.

The question is, however, will you keep it up? You may have gone to evening classes and then – along with two-thirds of the class – found yourself tailing off and abandoning the class in spite of your best intentions at the outset.

Changing habits isn't easy. Changing a lot of habits at the same time is even harder. That's why it's important to take one small, attainable step and practise and practise until it becomes a habit. In the 10 steps of this programme, there are hundreds of different things you could learn to do. To turn all of them into habits will take months – if not years. So this isn't a book that you can read once and hope to put into practice immediately.

Having read through this book, you need to *prioritise*. Below is a summary of some of the main types of action in the 10 steps. Put a tick opposite each one in terms of the level of priority you plan to give it.

	High	Medium	Low
Step 1: Measure your think-age			
Assess your think-age			
How old is your lifestyle?			
Step 2: Is your way of life ageing you?			
Assess the challenge in your life			
Assess the change in your life			
Assess the level of learning in your life			
Step 3: Make your challenge plan			
Work			
Sports/physical activity			
Interests			
Social life			
Entertainment			
Travel			
Step 4: Your change plan			
Do something you've never done before			
Change your appearance			
Change your physical activity level			
Talk to someone you've never talked to before			
Go to entertainment you've never encountered before			
Go somewhere you've never been before			
Do something on whim			
Change sleeping routine			
Break your lunchtime habit			

	High	Medium	Low
Step 5: Your learning plan			
New skill			
New language			
New knowledge			
Formal course			
Structured self-learning			
Belief system			
Self-oriented learning			
Local community			
Political/social/advocacy activities			
Step 6: Can you change?			
Do you believe you can change?			
Do you want to change?			
Step 7: Feed your brain: exercise and diet			
Make an exercise plan			
Improve your diet			
Step 8: Learn to relax and reduce stress			
Assess your stress			
Assess your goals			
Exert control			
Physical relaxation			
Autonomic relaxation			
Mental relaxation			
Step 9: Improve your memory			
Slide show			
Method of loci			
Pegword			
Multimedia (using other senses)			
BALL method			
Expanded rehearsal (test at increasing intervals)			
Mixing not maxing your learning			
Step 10: Manage your mind			
Pause			
Pose the question			
Put into words			
Mind management while reading			
Mind management in everyday life			

Now, from the list of actions that you consider to be of high priority, go back and read the relevant chapters of this book once more. Then choose the three that you will work on over the next week:

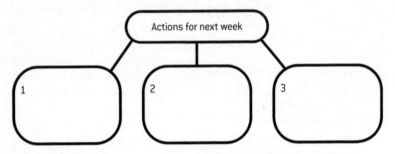

Once you have practised these actions repeatedly, you can move on to other elements of the programme. It is likely to take several weeks or even months before you notice the effects of the changes you make. But remember – it is all to play for – and if you put even a fraction of the effort into the challenge, change and learning in this stage of your life that you did in your youth, you will find your mental sharpness and your mental age improve. Good luck from one in his prime to all of you in yours.

References

1. Ball K, Berch DB, et al (2002) Effects of cognitive training interventions with older adults: A randomised controlled trial. *Journal of the American Medical Association* 13, 2271–2281.

2. Manly, T, K Hawkins, et al (2002). 'Rehabilitation of Executive Function: Facilitation of effective goal management on complex tasks using periodic auditory alerts.' *Neuropsychologia* **40**: 271–281; Manly, T, J Heutink, et al (2004). 'An electronic knot in the handkerchief: "Content free cueing" and the maintenance of attentive control.' *Neuropsychological Rehabilitation* **14**: 89–116; Robertson, IH (2002). 'Cognitive neuroscience and brain rehabilitation: a promise kept (Editorial).' *Journal of Neurology, Neurosurgery and Psychiatry* **73**: 357; Robertson, IH, JB Mattingley, et al (1998). 'Phasic alerting of neglect patients overcomes their spatial deficit in visual awareness.' *Nature* **395**(10): 169–172; Robertson, IH and JMJ Murre (1999). 'Rehabilitation of brain damage: Brain plasticity and principles of guided recovery.' *Psychological Bulletin* **125**: 544–575.

3. Robertson, Ian (2000) *Mind Sculpture*. London: Bantam.

4. Bargh JA, Chen M and Burrows L (1996) 'Automaticity of social behavior: Direct effects of trait construct and stereotype activation on action.' *Journal of Personality and Social Psychology* 71, 230–244.

5. *Journal of the American Medical Association*, Feb 13th, 2002, Wilson RS, et al.

6. Dawson, D, G Winocur, et al (1999). The psychosocial environment and cognitive rehabilitation in the elderly. *Cognitive Neurorehabilitation*. DT Stuss, G Winocur and IH Robertson. Cambridge, Cambridge University Press: 94–108.

7. Broadbent, DB, PF Cooper, et al (1982). 'The Cognitive Failures Questionnaire (CFQ) and its correlates.' *British Journal of Clinical Psychology* **21**: 1–16.

8. Churchill JD, et al (2002). 'Exercise, experience and the aging brain.' *Neurobiology of Aging* 23 (2002) 941–955; Bosma H, et al (2003). 'Mental work demands protect against cognitive impairment: MAAS prospective cohort study.' *Experimental Aging Research* 29: 33–45.

9. Bosma H, et al (2003). 'Mental work demands protect against cognitive impairment: MAAS prospective cohort study.' *Experimental Aging Research* 29: 33–45.

10. Ahissar, E, S Haidarliu, et al (1996). 'Possible involvement of neuromodulatory

systems in cortical Hebbian-like plasticity.' *Journal of Physiology-Paris* **90**: 353–360.

11. Bosma H, et al (2003). 'Mental work demands protect against cognitive impairment: MAAS prospective cohort study.' *Experimental Aging Research* 29: 33–45.

12. Gould, E, A Beylin, et al (1999). 'Learning enhances adult neurogenesis in the hippocampal formation.' *Nature Neuroscience* 2(3): 260–265.

13. Recanzone, GH, CE Schreiner, et al (1993). 'Plasticity in the frequency representation of primary auditory cortex.' *Journal of Neuroscience* **13**: 87–103.

14. Simons DJ and Levin DT (1998). 'Failure to detect changes to people during real-world interaction.' *Psychonomic Bulletin and Review* 4, 644–654.

15. Gould, E, A Beylin, et al (1999). 'Learning enhances adult neurogenesis in the hippocampal formation.' *Nature Neuroscience* 2(3): 260–265.

16. Bilingualism, Aging, and Cognitive Control: Evidence From the Simon Task E Bialystok, FIM Craik, R Klein, M Viswanathan. *Psychology and Aging* 2004, 19, 290–303.

17. Roche R, Robertson IH and O'Mara S (under review). Hippocampal and memory changes after rote learning training in elderly participants.

18. Churchill JD, Galvez, R, Colcombe S, Swain RA, Kramer, AC, Greenough WT (2002). 'Exercise, experience and. the aging brain.' *Neurobiology of Aging* 23, 941–955.

19. Dustman RE, Ruhling RO, Russell EM, Shearer DE, Bonekat W, Shigeoka JW, et al. 'Aerobic exercise training and improved neurophysiological function of older adults.' *Neurobiol Aging* 1984; 5:35–42.

20. Op cit

21. Rikli R, Edwards D. 'Effects of a 3-year exercise program on motor function and cognitive processing speed in older women.' *Res Q Exer Sport* 1991; 62:61–7.

22. Winocur, G and CE Greenwood (1999). 'The effects of high fat diets and environmental influences on cognitive performance in rats [In Process Citation].' *Behav Brain Res* 101(2): 153–61.

23. Grady CL et al. *Science* 269: (5221) 218–221 Jul 14 1995.

24. Buckner R. Paper presented at the International Congress on Psychology, Stockholm, 2000.

25. Ball K, Berch DB, et al (2002). 'Effects of cognitive training interventions with older adults: A randomised controlled trial.' *Journal of the American Medical Association* 13, 2271–2281.

26. Denis M (1982). 'Imaging while reading text: a study of individual differences.' *Memory and Cognition* 10, 540–5.

27. Paivio A and Csapo K (1973). 'Picture superiority in free recall.' *Cognitive Psychology* 5, 176–206.

28. Nickerson RS (1999). 'Enhancing Creativity.' In RJ Sternberg (ed) *Handbook of Creativity*. Cambridge: Cambridge University Press, 392–430.

29. Baer JM (1988). 'Long-term effects of creativity training with middle-school students.' *Journal of Early Adolescence* 8, 183–193.

30. Adey P and Shayer M (1993). 'An exploration of long-term transfer effects following an extended intervention program in the High School science curriculum.' *Cognition and Instruction* 11, 1–29.

31. Bjork RA, & Bjork EL (1992). 'A new theory of disuse and an old theory of stimulus fluctuation.' In A Healy, S Kosslyn, & R Shiffrin (Eds.), *From learning processes to cognitive processes: Essays in honor of William K. Estes* (Vol. 2, pp. 35–67). Hillsdale, NJ: Erlbaum.

32. Melcher JM, et al (1996). 'The misremembrance of wines past: Verbal and perceptual expertise differentially mediate verbal overshadowing of taste memory.' *Journal of Memory and Language* 35, 231–245.

33. Levine, B, I Robertson, et al (2000). 'Rehabilitation of executive functioning: An experimental-clinical validation of Goal Management Training.' *Journal of the International Neuropsychological Society*; O'Connor, C, T Manly, et al (2004). 'An fMRI study of sustained attention with endogenous and exogenous engagement.' *Brain and Cognition* **54**: 133–135.

34. Op Cit.

35. Einstein A (1952). Letter to Jacque Hadamard. In B. Ghiselin (Ed) *The Creative Process* (pp. 43–44). Berkeley: University of California Press.

Index